D1596895

The
Garland Library
of
War and Peace

The
Garland Library
of
War and Peace

Under the General Editorship of
Blanche Wiesen Cook, *John Jay College, C.U.N.Y.*
Sandi E. Cooper, *Richmond College, C.U.N.Y.*
Charles Chatfield, *Wittenberg University*

Bryan
and
World Peace

by
Merle Eugene Curti

with a new Introduction
for the Garland Edition by
Merle Eugene Curti

Garland Publishing, Inc., New York & London
1971

Introduction

In an essay on Bryan's diplomacy that appeared in 1968, Professor Richard Challener generously referred to Bryan and World Peace, *published thirty-seven years earlier, as "the most useful study of Bryan's foreign policy." I felt justified in saying, in a foreword to the 1969 reprinting of my monograph, that it was still the most complete account of the Great Commoner's relationship to the problem of war and peace. This is no longer the case. Paolo E. Coletta's second volume of his biography,* William Jennings Bryan: Progressive Politician and Moral Statesman 1909-1915, *is now by far the most thoroughly researched and detailed account of the testing of Bryan's commitment to peace during the years when he was Wilson's Secretary of State. Thus a few words of explanation for another reprinting of my early study seem in order.*

In the scholarship of American foreign relations the "realist" school has regarded Bryan's role as Secretary of State as an example of an over-reliance on moralistic rhetoric and exhortation with the failure to assess the relationship of what was said to national interest and to a willingness, if need be, of invoking force to implement words. Writing long before the full impact of "realist" scholarship I did

5

INTRODUCTION

*not use its idiom. But I did see some of the obstacles
that prevented the implementation of Bryan's basic
tenet,namely, the adoption of a single standard of
morality for both interpersonal and international
relations, the standard expressed in the belief in the
universal validity of the Golden Rule, Christian love
and brotherhood, and the common sense maxim that
"nothing can be final among friends." Bryan did not
fully recognize the obstacles that the distribution and
use of power on the international stage posed to his
oversimplified formula. Nor did he fully recognize
the relationship between the American sense of
mission to remake the world in the image of
democracy and the pull of intervention in the
European conflict. His own devotion to his principles
and to his party chief finally led him, not to
compromise in order to keep his office, but to resign
and to take his case to the nation. When war finally
came he supported it out of a deep sense of
patriotism.*

*On the other hand, in recognizing the limitations
of Bryan's pacifism in an operative situation, it is easy
to underestimate its strength. A completely negative
case cannot be sustained for Bryan's "utopianism" in
the matter of his famous "cooling off" treaties. The
principle of delaying an appeal to arms while an
investigating commission reported the facts in the
conflict has been advantageously used in the United
Nations' peace-keeping efforts. Nor was Bryan's
adaptation of his peace commitment to the complex*

and tangled problems in the Caribbean and the Far East entirely unrealistic. It is true that the increasingly stiff objections to Japan's "Twenty-One Demands" on China could not, short of evidence of the willingness to use force, greatly alter the situation. It is also true that in supporting Wilson's use of force in Mexico and in his own calling for a naval demonstration in Haiti, Bryan was hardly acting the role of an exponent of the Golden Rule. On the other hand, he advocated the substitution of public for private loans for the development of the economies of Latin American countries in the interest of limiting the profit motive in imperialism. Though rejected at the time, this has become a national policy. Bryan's paternalistic sense of the national mission to strengthen the American conception of order and democracy did not fit the realities in Central America and the Caribbean countries. Yet the motives of good will and helpfulness that governed his interventions differed from the motives that operated in earlier and later instances of American imperialistic intervention. Latin Americans appreciated the difference even though the resulting actions did not lead to essentially different results. When world war broke out in 1914 Bryan, more than Wilson or any other highly placed official, was, thanks to his commitment to Christian ethics and to a measure of common sense, the most truly neutral and nonpartisan figure in the Administration. Some of his proposals were later adopted by Wilson (the offer to mediate) and by

7

INTRODUCTION

Congress (the neutrality legislation of the 1930s). That these proposals and laws did not achieve their ends when tried does not prove that this would have necessarily been the case had Bryan been able to persuade Wilson to adopt his views in 1914 and 1915.

Thus on balance Bryan's record was neither "realistic" nor "utopian" but a mixture of the two, with loyalty to the principle of peace triumphing over expediency in the final crisis that led to his resignation.

A re-reading of Bryan and World Peace *bears out, I believe, such an interpretation, one similar to that of Professor Coletta. The student who wishes a detailed and thoroughly documented account, based on many materials not available in 1931, must read Coletta's admirable biography. But my shorter monograph may be useful, both because of its relationship in time to the whole historiography of the subject and because it reflects, I believe, more sharply than a longer, very detailed account easily can, the high tension and tragic sense of what happened when a committed devotee of peace experienced the limitations imposed on his commitment by factors that were beyond his control.*

Madison, 1971   Merle Curti
                                        Department of History
                                        University of Wisconsin

Vol. XVI, Nos. 3-4   April-July, 1931

Smith College Studies in History

JOHN C. HILDT
WILLIAM DODGE GRAY
HAROLD UNDERWOOD FAULKNER
Editors

BRYAN AND WORLD PEACE

by

MERLE EUGENE CURTI

NORTHAMPTON, MASS.
Published Quarterly by the Department of History of Smith College
Entered as second-class matter December 14, 1915, at the postoffice at Northampton
Mass., under the act of August 24, 1912

CONTENTS

FOREWORD

The story of Bryan's relation to the institution of war and the efforts to prevent it has been told by his biographers only in a fragmentary way. While it is perhaps too soon to evaluate definitively the contributions Bryan made to the peace movement, it is hoped that this study, based in large part on the *Bryan Papers* in the Library of Congress, may help illuminate Bryan's personality as well as contribute a chapter to the history of the peace movement.

I wish especially to express my gratitude to Mrs. Mary Baird Bryan for permission to use the *Bryan Papers,* and to Mrs. W. W. Bailey and the Reverend Charles Macfarland for sending me copies of Bryan letters in their possession. Dr. George Kirchwey also kindly cleared up for me one or two interesting points. I am indebted to Miss Eunice Schuster for some helpful suggestions made in a seminar paper on Bryan and his peace treaties.

I should like to take this opportunity to thank the John Simon Guggenheim Foundation for making possible this study, the material for which was collected while I was a Guggenheim Fellow in 1929-1930.

I

BRYAN BECOMES AN ADVOCATE OF PEACE

The story of William Jennings Bryan's fight against war is a pathetic one. He loved peace, labored arduously for it, and dearly prized his achievements in its behalf; and yet he fought in one war, was responsible, with President McKinley, for fastening on the country a treaty which inaugurated our imperialism, sister of war and mother of navies; and, at his own request, was buried with military honors in the national cemetery at Arlington. It is not these contradictions alone, however, which make Bryan's war against war a pathetic story. It is rather the essential futility of the struggle, which was not only his struggle, but that of thousands of others whose feelings and ideas he expressed. For, in spite of certain victories, that struggle might be judged a failure. In the light of Bryan's social philosophy and that of the simple, rural folk whom he represented so well, it is an illuminating failure. Considered in relation to the shifting currents of the economic and political life of America, Bryan's pacifism transcends the personal and group equation, and assumes a sort of epic significance. For in a very real sense the stand which this moral leader took on militarism, imperialism and world peace represents at the same time all that was finest and all that was weakest and most ineffective in the peace movement of yesterday, and, more than many are willing to admit, in that of today. And a survey of Bryan's labors for peace, set against a larger background, may clarify in some measure, at least, the problem of determining the influence and limitations of the reformer in public life.

Bryan was the product of an older America which during the whole of his life was rapidly giving way to a new and different country, an America he only very vaguely understood. Frontier and rural America was competing ever less successfully with industrial and urban America; church-believing America was becoming secularized; and new empires for the dominant business groups were sought and obtained, together with an efficient navy to insure advantages to bankers and industrialists.   These changes did not take place unchallenged: it was Bryan's fortune to lead the old forces against the new.   Perhaps it was as hopeless a task as that of the Southern planters who went down to defeat before industrialism when Lee surrendered at Appomattox; perhaps a wiser and more skillful leader could have done no more than retard, without preventing, the final triumph of the new order.   Yet Bryan's stubborn devotion to his party sometimes defeated his own ends, or made their defeat the more likely; and his over-simplified analyses of and solutions for problems sometimes, by blinding his eyes to their complex character, lessened the force of the blows he struck against the new order.   Of its evils none were more evident than militarism and imperialism: Bryan saw his country engage in two wars, acquire an empire, and build a huge navy.   To all this he was as much opposed as he was to the decline of faith in orthodox religion, the gold standard, the trusts, and the rule of the "plutocracy."

There was little that was original in this crusader's philosophy of peace.   His aversion to "wholesale blood-letting", his conviction that war was unchristian, and that there was a better means than force for solving international problems, came to him only very gradually.   The seeds of his pacifism were sown in his boyhood; the Spanish-American war, and, more particularly, the imperialism which seemed to result from it, marked an important step in its development; and finally, his visit to Tolstoy in 1903 quickened and confirmed his faith in love as an effective alternative to force.

Deeply religious, Bryan had been taught at his mother's knee that all men are brothers, and that the first Christian duty is to love one's neighbors.   It is indeed not clear at just what point he came to vision universal brotherhood as the goal of nations, and the golden rule as the chief means to that end.   It had at least occurred to him by 1879—he was then nineteen.   "The sound of armor, the glittering steel and the gory field of battle" had no charm for him, and he was convinced—so he wrote his cousin, Thomas Marshall, of Salem, Illinois—that the time was swiftly passing by when armies ruled. "The dawn of a brighter day is at hand. Right is beginning to take the place of might."[1] Perhaps he was associating his Christian precepts with public events which had only recently come to his attention—the withdrawal of federal troops from the South. Or possibly he had heard of the victory for international arbitration in the Geneva award. Or, who knows, he might have stumbled on one of the tracts which the agent of the American Peace Society in Chicago had been scattering over his native state. But if he had so early formulated a consistent and definite philosophy, his papers have left no record of it. The years that followed were busy years; years of struggle in establishing a law practice, in building up a political reputation in Nebraska, and in dramatizing the silver issue. Yet during all this time he did not forget the precepts of his boyhood—precepts which had become, and were to remain, the cornerstone of his later pacifism.

Inspired by Christian ethics, Bryan's philosophy of peace was nourished by faith in American individualism and popular government. Americans in his youth, like those of an earlier and later time, were thinking in terms of individualism. Jefferson knew of but "one code of morality for men, whether acting singly or collectively," and Bryan marked well this precept. Once he became concerned with international problems, he carried over into that field of thought the conviction that the behavior of nations was exactly analogous to that of individuals. When passion brought two men to the point of fighting, the remedy was obviously to keep them apart until their claims and charges might be investigated, and their controversy calmly discussed.[2] The same rule should apply to nations. If this idea overlooked the fact that the

---

[1] Mary Baird Bryan, *The Memoirs of William Jennings Bryan*, (Philadelphia, 1925), 383.

[2] For a striking example of the way in which Bryan carried this idea from an individual to a general application see "The Forces that Make for Peace", *Report of the Sixteenth Annual Meeting of the Lake Mohonk Conference*, 1910, 170.

behavior of nations is far more complex than that of individuals, the analogy was none the less entirely natural for one who had grown up in rural America only a generation away from the old frontier. Such a conviction, indeed, was deeply rooted in an intensely individualistic outlook and way of life.

Closely associated with this point of view was Bryan's faith in democracy—his conviction that democracy was identical with progress, and that the spread of popular government throughout the world would mean the victory of international peace. He had no doubt that war was part and parcel of monarchies and aristocracies, and that militarism and popular government were incompatible. The burden of war always fell on the masses; but now, since democracy everywhere was replacing aristocracy, they could and would protest against being slaughtered for some one else's interest.[3]

Sharing as he did with hundreds of thousands of Americans these basic sources of pacifism—faith in Christianity and in an individualistic democracy—Bryan could not claim any originality for his philosophy of peace. Nor was there, as we shall see, very much that was new in his specific program to prevent war.[4] None the less his contribution to the peace movement was an original one. He may indeed never have read Emerson's observation that "the power of love, as the basis of a State, has never been tried." His claim to originality, as far as the peace movement is concerned, lies in the fact that he was the first man in public office to try to put such a doctrine into practice.[5] He was a pioneer among statesmen in taking up the work of earlier peace advocates and in attempting to translate it into terms of political action. In trying to apply to the affairs of nations this high ideal of love as the basis of a state, he was unquestionably sincere and courageous if not always consistent.

When the inflammatory propaganda for a war with Spain

[3] *Ibid.*, 166.
[4] *Post.* 144.
[5] It is true that William Penn was in part guided by this philosophy in his New World experiment.

swept the country, Bryan (not yet a pacifist, one must remember), enthusiastically waved a Cuban flag at a Jeffersonian banquet, declaring that the United States ought to intervene for Cuban independence.[6] It was generally recognized that intervention meant war, which the administration was still trying, nominally at least, to avert. Far from endeavoring to stem the popular clamor, Bryan blessed it. His voice was the voice of the frontiersman speaking for self-determination, for popular sovereignty; it was the cry of the leader of an oppressed agrarian population sympathizing with the struggling underdogs on neighboring soil; and, in the excited clamor for intervention, it was not bad politics. Asked by a representative of the Omaha *World-Herald* whether in his judgment the time had come to intervene in Cuba, Bryan made clear his position:

"Humanity demands that we should act. . . . War is a terrible thing and cannot be defended except as a means to an end, and yet it is sometimes the only means by which a necessary end can be secured. The state punishes its own citizens by imprisonment and even death when counsel and persuasion fail; war is the final arbiter between nations when reason and diplomacy are of no avail."[7]

Ignorant of the fact that diplomacy and reason could easily have won all that we asked of Spain, Bryan, on the day war was declared, offered his services to President McKinley for any duty to which he might be assigned.[8] President McKinley ignored his telegram. But Bryan enlisted as a private, and later, by the authority of the governor of Nebraska, raised a regiment,[9] convinced that

". . . universal peace cannot come until Justice is enthroned throughout the world. . . . Until the right has triumphed in every land and love reigns supreme in every heart, government must, as a last resort, appeal to force. As long as the oppressor

---

[6] Arthur Wallace Dunn, *From Harrison to Harding*, (N. Y. and London, 1922), I, 236-7. Bryan's speech was referred to in the Senate, where a Democrat said that Mr. Bryan's voice was the command of six million Democrats who had voted for him in 1896. Dunn, *op. cit.*, 237.

[7] *Bryan Papers*, 29, (no date).

[8] *Ibid.*, 34, Lincoln, Apr. 25, 1898, telegram to President McKinley.

[9] *Memoirs of William Jennings Bryan*, 119-120.

is deaf to the voice of reason, so long must the citizen accustom his shoulder to the musket and his hand to the saber."[10]

Bryan went to war. The man for whom military claptrap had no charm at the age of nineteen now, wearing the new uniform on which his wife had tearfully stitched the necessary insignia, took command of his regiment, flashing his sword into the sunlight of a hot July day. Far from betraying his principles, he was a crusader: he had never condemned a holy war.

Bryan went to war. The spirit was willing, but the flesh was weak: he was no soldier. Great democrat that everyone knew him to be, he might have been forgiven for fraternizing with the men under his command. Moreover, his superiors commended him for the admirable condition of his command.[11] But he was haunted by fears—not, indeed, fears of battle, but fears of the political consequences of battle! Distressed particularly by the fear that the war, instead of merely bringing freedom to Cuba, might end by enslaving the Filipinos, he wondered whether he might not better be in civilian life combating this new menace. In the army silence—military lockjaw he called it—was the order of the day. But "Their's not to reason why; their's but to do and die" had little meaning for him. Nor was it alone the politician and statesman in him that kept him from being a good soldier. It was somehow not at all in his make-up to be one. Unable to grasp the idea that the sole business of the soldier is to kill, he thought, rather, it was his function to sacrifice his life for his country, his ideal, and for God.[12] "The essence of patriotism", he had said in a memorial address at Arlington cemetery four years earlier, "lies in a willingness to sacrifice for one's country, just as true greatness finds expression, not in blessings enjoyed, but in good bestowed." What made the soldier truly glorious was that he,

[10] New York *Times,* June 15, 1898, *The Second Battle* (Chicago, 1900), 85. This was said at the Trans-Mississippi Exposition, Omaha, June 14, 1898.

[11] Boston *Daily Globe,* Dec. 16, 1898.

[12] Bryan to Carnegie, Lincoln, Jan. 13, 1899, *Bryan Papers, 27;* *Speeches,* (N. Y. and London, 1913), II, 192; Paxton Hibben, *The Peerless Leader,* (N. Y., 1929), 216-217.

like Christ, "yielded up for the welfare of his fellows life's most precious blood."[13] After all, had he not been taught at his mother's knee, and had he ever really doubted that all men are truly brethren? Was it not written that he who ruleth his own spirit is greater than he who taketh the city? Were not the meek to inherit the earth? Was it not better to give than to receive, to sacrifice one's blood rather than to take that of one's brother? Was not, in short, His way the noblest way to glory? But it was not for Bryan to reap glory in the fever-ridden camps of Florida, nor from the abusive Republican press. The war might make a political fortune for Roosevelt; it made none for him.

But the war did turn his potential pacifism into concrete channels. Its fruit was imperialism, and for this Bryan had no heart.. Even before he was sworn into the service, he had sensed the danger that the war might end in colonial expansion, and before any other public man, had announced his opposition to imperialism.[14] Without fully understanding the reasons, probably, Bryan felt that imperialism could only make richer and more powerful the America of industry and finance, against which he had fought—and lost—the First Great Battle.

"When trade is secured by force, the cost of securing it and retaining it must be taken out of the profits, and the profits are never large enough to cover the expense. Such a system would never be defended but for the fact that the expense is borne by all the people, while the profits are enjoyed by a few. Imperialism would be profitable to the ship owners, who would be able to carry live soldiers to the Philippines and bring dead soldiers back; it would be profitable to those who would seize upon the franchises, and it would be profitable to the officials whose salaries would be fixt here and paid over there; but to the farmer, to the laboring man and to the vast majority of those engaged in other occupations it would bring expenditure without return and risk without reward."[15] . . . "Imperialism finds its inspiration in dollars, not in duty. It is not our duty to burden our people with increased

---

[13] *The Second Battle*, 80.
[14] *Memoirs of William Jennings Bryan*, 120; *The Second Battle*, 84 ff.
[15] *Speeches of William Jennings Bryan*, II, 42.

taxes in order to give a few speculators an opportunity for exploitation."[16]

It did not take this Middle Westerner long to see that Philippine sugar would weaken his agrarian allies by competing with the product of the Colorado beet growers and the Louisiana cane planters. He perceived, too, that immigration from the Philippines would lower the living standards of America workers: in short, that imperialism would weaken the masses economically, and strengthen the already powerful, possessing classes.

Yet it was really on moral and political grounds, rather than on economic, that Bryan fought expansion. He believed that all men were created equal, despite the fact that he had done little to persuade Southern Democrats to recognize that Jeffersonian doctrine in their treatment of negroes. He really thought that governments derived their powers from the governed, though, in a more realistic moment, he had once perceived that the power of wealth controlled the government. To retain the Philippines, he felt, was to repudiate our political philosophy of self-government and equality before the law. "We cannot repudiate the principle of self-government in the Philippines without weakening that principle here."[17] Imperialism was clearly a step backward, towards "the narrow views of kings and emperors," and the fruits of imperialism, bitter and sweet, had better be left to the subjects of monarchy. Repudiated by our forefathers in 1776, imperialism had recrossed the seas, was challenging our democracy, threatening it with such evils as militarism, navalism and entanglements in the disputes of foreign powers. These were grave evils—so grave that they menaced the Republic itself.

Nor did Bryan have any sympathy with the argument that it was our duty to acquire an empire in order to Christianize it. There was no Bible warrant whatever for imperialism, and he

---

[16] *The Second Battle,* 91. (Speech delivered before the Nebraska Traveling Men's Club banquet, Lincoln, Dec. 31, 1898.) Bryan's economic indictment is to be contrasted with Henry Cabot Lodge's defense of imperialism on economic grounds.

[17] *Speeches,* II, 24.

compared the "swaggering, bullying, brutal doctrine of imperialism" with the golden rule and the commandment, "Thou shalt
love thy neighbor as thyself." Who could say we had any divine
command to civilize the Filipinos "with dynamite and proselyte
with the sword?" As for our missionaries, it was to be hoped
that they were seeking souls rather than sovereignty, and the
Nazarene's way of reaching human hearts was through love,
through sacrifice for others, and not through their exploitation.[18]

Such was Bryan's indictment of imperialism, an indictment
carried persuasively and sincerely over the length and breadth
of the land. Yet his behavior in the battle over the ratification
of the treaty by which the war with Spain was ended and by
which we acquired the Philippines subjected him to the criticism
that he, more than any person except President McKinley himself, was responsible for fastening on the country the very imperialism he so heartily denounced.

Before resigning his commission on December 12, 1898, Bryan
had observed, with no little regret, the widespread enthusiasm for
expansion, an enthusiasm shared by many Democrats. It was to
oppose this sentiment that, the very day after putting on civilian
clothing, he declared, in an interview at Savannah, his opposition
to imperialism. Yet to the surprise of the anti-imperialists who
were opposing the treaty which made America sovereign over
the Philippines, Bryan favored its ratification:

"It will be easier, I think, to end the war at once by ratifying the
treaty and then deal with the subject in our own way. The issue
can be presented directly by a resolution to Congress declaring the
policy of the nation upon the subject. The President in his message says that our only purpose in taking possession of Cuba is to
establish a stable government and then turn that government over
to the people of Cuba. Congress could reaffirm this purpose in
regard to Cuba and assert the same purpose in regard to the
Philippines and Porto Rico."[19]

[18] *Ibid.*, 43 ff.
[19] *The Second Battle,* 88. Interview at Savannah, Dec. 13, 1898; *Memoirs
of William Jennings Bryan,* 120; Bryan to Carnegie, Lincoln, Neb., Jan. 13,
1899, *Bryan Papers,* 27; A. W. Dunn, *From Harrison to Harding,* I, 282-3.

Hurrying on to Washington, the Democratic leader urged his political supporters in Congress to support the treaty together with a declaration of our purpose to grant independence to the Philippines. It was certain that Bryan could have prevented the ratification of the treaty and our acquisition of the archipelago. While Senator Pettigrew indignantly refused to change front and vote for the treaty when urged to do so, some of Bryan's supporters did as he advised them.[20] Bryan's influence is brought out in letters and telegrams from Andrew Carnegie, who was in Washington endeavoring to defeat the treaty because of his opposition to imperialism:

Washington, Jan. 10, 1899.
"Friends here who know tell me the treaty can be defeated with 2 or 3 votes to spare. Your advocacy of ratification has discouraged matters—several are now shaky against defeating it. You know of course that one vote in the pass is worth two in the open. I wish you were here to be satisfied that you have the power to defeat this Treaty. . . . Our friends say the situation looks better but the two leaders separately said to me today that we were all right until Bryan came."[21]

The next day Carnegie pleaded with Bryan by telegraph to acquiesce in plans of his followers to vote with Democratic leaders against ratification, adding

"Our friends assure me votes were secured to defeat the treaty, but your advice shakes several."[22]

Bryan, admitting that he had tried to convince Democratic senators but denying that he controlled them, adhered to his course.[23] Other appeals from political friends in Washington begging him to

[20] R. F. Pettigrew, *Imperial Washington,* (Chicago, 1922), 270. Although Senator Jones of Arkansas maintained that Bryan did not change a vote, it seems very probable that he influenced Senator Allen of Nebraska and Senator Jones of Nevada to support the treaty. Erving Winslow, an officer of the Anti-Imperialist League and an associate of Bryan in the campaign of 1900, thought that Bryan's interviews in Washington "undoubtedly weakened the party opposition to the treaty." *The Independent,* LI, May 18, 1899, 1348-1349.
[21] *Bryan Papers,* 27.
[22] *Ibid.,* Carnegie to Bryan, Washington, Jan. 11, 1899.
[23] *Ibid.,* Bryan to Carnegie, Lincoln, Jan. 11, 1899.

support those who were trying to defeat or amend the treaty, were equally fruitless.[24] Urgent appeals continued to come. On January 17th a Democratic senator, regretting that Bryan had favored ratification, informed him that the treaty could easily be amended.[25] Bryan stood his ground. And as late as January 20 Senator H. M. Teller, who agreed with him in favoring ratification, wrote that the situation was not encouraging, since Gorman seemed to have captured enough Democratic votes to defeat the treaty.[26] Until the final, narrow victory—the treaty was ratified with only one vote to spare—Democratic senators, with certain Republicans, hoped to defeat the administration forces on the treaty, and persisted in trying to persuade Bryan to support their efforts.

Other evidence confirms the impression that Bryan might easily have prevented the ratification of the treaty.[27] Senator George F. Hoar, one of the ablest Republicans opposing it, wrote to Bryan:

"I felt very sure of the defeat of the treaty, with a good many votes to spare. In that condition of things I was told, not by one or two or three only, but by a considerable number of influential Democrats, your political friends and supporters, who had supported you for the Presidency at the last election and expected to do so again, that you came to Washington, and, in spite of an earnest remonstrance from them, urged persons whom you could influence to vote for the treaty. The result was, as I understand it, that a considerable number of persons who had in private—but without secrecy—declared their opposition to the treaty, voted for it, and it was carried by one vote to spare, although one of those gentlemen withheld his vote until after the roll-call was over and the list of votes read and with the purpose of voting against the treaty if he could thereby defeat it, unless he thought some advan-

[24] Wilkinson Call (Senator from Florida) telegram to Bryan, Washington, Jan. 12, 1899.

[25] U. S. Senate, Jan. 17, 1899—unsigned.

[26] H. M. Teller to Bryan, Washington, Jan. 20, 1899, *Bryan Papers*, 27.

[27] Senator James K. Jones of Arkansas insisted that Bryan's fear that Spain might revive the war if the treaty were defeated was groundless, and that if the treaty were ratified "Elkins and Hanna would simply say we have ratified the treaty with your help, have transferred the sovereignty to the United States, and will let the matter rest where it is." Jones to Bryan, Jan. 20, 1899, *Bryan Papers*, 27.

tages would come from it. The result was the greatest single disappointment of my political life.[28] . . . I cannot help thinking that, next to President McKinley, you are the person in the country most responsible for the adoption of the treaty, and for the lamentable occurrences that have happened since the war with that innocent people (the Filipinos). . . ."

Senator Hoar thought that it would not have been difficult to amend the treaty, had it been defeated, so as to put the Philippines on the same footing as Cuba. Spain was utterly vanquished, without hope, and would promptly have agreed to such an amendment.

Why did Bryan, sincere anti-imperialist that he was, refuse to exert his influence to prevent our acquisition of the Philippines? It has been generally held that his motive in favoring the treaty was a desire to create a popular issue for the Democratic party in the campaign of 1900,—to enable it to condemn the imperialism inaugurated under a Republican administration. In his *Autobiography*, Andrew Carnegie reports that while in Washington for the purpose of defeating the treaty, he was told that Bryan had "advised his friends that it would be good party policy to allow the treaty to pass."[29] Senator Pettigrew maintained that Bryan's chief argument when he tried to persuade him to support the treaty was that the Republicans should and would be driven from power if they undertook to conquer the Islands and annex them to the United States.[30] And Senator Hoar has testified that Bryan told his supporters in Washington that "the Democratic Party could not hope to win a victory on the financial questions at stake after they had been beaten on them in a time of adversity; and that they must have this issue for the coming campaign."[31] There is additional evidence, nearer in point of time to the events, which supports the testimony of Carnegie, Pettigrew and Hoar. Clark Howell, a member of the Democratic National Committee, wrote

[28] Senator Hoar to Bryan, May 15, 1900, *Bryan Papers*, 27; George F. Hoar, *Autobiography of Seventy Years*, (N. Y., 1903) II, 322-323.
[29] Andrew Carnegie, *Autobiography* (Boston and N. Y., 1920), 363.
[30] R. F. Pettigrew, *Imperial Washington*, 270.
[31] George F. Hoar, *Autobiography of Seventy Years*, II, 322-323.

from Washington to the Atlanta *Constitution* on December 20, 1898, that Bryan advised ratification of the treaty, not only because of national obligation but also because of party policy.[32] Such, also, was the opinion expressed in the newspapers of the day. Such opposition papers as the New York *Tribune*[33] were not alone in believing that he was playing politics. The Springfield *Republican* wrote on December 15:

"That Mr. Bryan anticipates fighting some political battles over imperialism is evident from his readiness to let the treaty be ratified, thus throwing, as he calculates, the whole question into the political arena."[34]

This, too, was the interpretation put on his policy by the New York *Evening Post,*[35] while the Hartford *Courant* declared that he was adding another string to his political bow, so that the Democratic Convention might nominate him as an anti-empire man if it did not choose to do so as an anti-gold man.[36]

Bryan, indeed, was too shrewd a politician to miss a good opportunity for promoting the interest of his party. There is, however, evidence in the Bryan papers and in other contemporary accounts which indicates that motives other than a mere desire to create a new, popular issue for the Democratic party played an important part in Bryan's support of the treaty. In the first place he was not convinced that imperialism was the most important issue for his party to oppose. Indeed there was considerable enthusiasm for it among the Democrats. Important newspapers, particularly the Atlanta *Constitution,* the New York *Journal,* and the Washington *Times* had been loudly advocating expansion; and considerable pressure had been put on Bryan by Democratic imperialists to acquiesce in the policy of expansion.[37] At the very time that Bryan was in Washington, President McKinley, with a justification for expansion on his tongue, was being received

[32] New York *Tribune,* Dec. 22, 1898.
[33] New York *Tribune,* Dec. 26, 1898.
[34] Springfield *Republican,* Dec. 15, 1898.
[35] Cited in the Springfield *Republican,* Dec. 15, 1898.
[36] *Ibid.*
[37] Springfield *Republican,* Dec. 15, 1898.

in the South with unprecedented and unexpected enthusiasm. Well might Bryan hesitate to urge anti-imperialism as the paramount issue when it was so obvious to everyone that his own party was far from being united on it.[38] Then too, both Bryan and a very important wing of the party still considered the free silver issue the vital one. On December 11, before Bryan had been released from the army, a poll taken among Democratic senators and congressmen in Washington indicated that the great body of the party's representatives at the capital preferred the old issues of 1896 to any new ones.[39] When reporters asked Bryan, the day of his arrival in Washington, what the issues of 1900 were likely to be, he did not hesitate to put silver before everything else:

"I should say the money question undoubtedly. I believe the Chicago platform still embodies the sentiments of the mass of the American people. I can see no reason for a popular change of mind on any of the issues defined in the last national platform. . . . The fact that the people are talking about war does not necessarily indicate that they have abandoned former ideas which have no reference to the war. People can discuss matters of temporary interest without forgetting their political views and abandoning their political principles."[40]

Three days later in New York he again upheld the same position. With hostilities at an end, he thought, the people could soberly resume discussion of domestic issues, of which free silver came first in importance.[41] Other political leaders at this time announced that this would be the dominant issue in the campaign of 1900.[42] True, Bryan continued to denounce imperialism; and he named anti-imperialism as the issue second in importance when pressed to outline the party's probable platform in the coming campaign.[43]

[38] Boston *Globe,* Dec. 20, 1898. A well-informed Washington correspondent, A. Maurice Low, reported that Southern representatives in Washington, and Bryan himself, were amazed at the reception given in the South to McKinley's imperialistic speeches. "It is believed here that Mr. Bryan saw the handwriting on the wall, interpreted it correctly, and as a result advised Democrats of the Senate not to oppose ratification."
[39] Boston *Globe,* Dec. 12, 1898.
[40] Boston *Globe,* Dec. 15, 1898.
[41] *Ibid.,* Dec. 18, 1898; Springfield *Republican,* Dec. 18, 1898.
[42] Boston *Globe,* Dec. 21, 1898.
[43] Springfield *Republican,* Dec. 18, 1898.

On his homecoming in Nebraska, the Peerless Leader reiterated his belief that the American people had not accepted the gold standard; that gold had been responsible for ills far worse than those Spain inflicted on Cuba; and that the trusts were ever so much more merciless than Weyler had ever been.[44]

And all this Bryan sincerely believed. When tempting inducements were made to persuade him to abandon free silver, and to concentrate on anti-imperialism, he turned deaf ears to his tempters. Of these, none was as interesting and persuasive and insistent as Andrew Carnegie. On the very morning of the announcement that Bryan had come out squarely against the permanent retention of the Philippines, the iron master of Pittsburgh congratulated him warmly on his position.[45]

Dec. 15, 1898, N. Y.

Your clear and most timely expression of views this morning impels me to write to say that in this hour of grave danger to Republican Institutions all partizanship fades away. We must get down to the solid body of patriotism which stands only for the Repub. & draws men of all parties & creeds & colors together in one solid man. True as I know you will be to the American idea you may rest assured that such a reaction is imminent as will sweep away all opposition. The American people have never failed to decide wisely. The uproar of war exciting the baser propensities for a time makes the issue difficult at first, but it will all come out right. There are hundreds of thousands in our party who will vote for the American as against any Imperialist. I am one of these. Labor is already against Imperialism and I look to the farmer to be heard from. Holding out to you the hand of fellowship in the new issue before us & wishing you god-speed—

Andrew Carnegie.

Bryan and Carnegie talked of the cause they both had at heart—"saving our country from the entanglements of the wars of Europe." The great industrialist determined to further the cause of anti-imperialism by persuading the champion of the masses to center all his efforts in that single cause, and, above all, to abandon the heresy of 1896:

Dec. 18

"I see you stick to silver. Well—let me tell you that it is the only superfluous load you *may* take and probably wreck your party.

[44] Boston *Globe*, Dec. 24, 1898.
[45] *Bryan Papers*, 27. Carnegie to Bryan.

No silver man can hope to carry New York. . . . I see in you with all your elements of popularity, your ability—a formidable candidate for the next presidential campaign. Only however if you see the one issue—the saving of the Republic from departure from its foundation principles. I see only this and am willing to subordinate all issues to it, but if we have to carry the silver question, then we are defeated from the start."[46]

Rumor of so strange an entente, or prospective entente, did not pass unnoticed in the press. Many of Bryan's friends were jubilant at the prospect of support from so wealthy and influential a man as Andrew Carnegie.[47] "When silver and iron fuse and join forces *versus* imperialism" observed the Boston *Globe*, "it's about time to reckon that something unusual is getting ready to drop."[48] But Arthur Brisbane of the New York *Journal* refused to print the story of an alliance between the two, and immediately warned Bryan of the dangers of any association whatever with the "promoter of the Homestead riots."[49] Turning down Brisbane's offer to silence Carnegie by an injunction if he insisted on talking about the New York interview, Bryan took his chances with the Scotchman. He lost no time in telegraphing him that he hoped the report that he had prepared for publication an account of their interview was untrue; and then, in decisive terms, he chose between free silver and anti-imperialism:

"I have not discussed the interview publicly and prefer that you do not. I am not a candidate for any office at this time. Whether I ever shall be again, depends upon circumstances. I not only ask no pledge of support, conditional or unconditional, but believe a pledge or prophecy likely to injure the cause of constitutional government against imperialism—a cause which is more dear to me than political preferment. I am making this fight in my own way and *hope to see the question disposed of before 1900*, so the fight against trusts and for free silver may be continued. You and I agree in opposing militarism and imperialism, but when these questions are settled we may find ourselves upon opposite sides as heretofore. Let us fight together when we can, and against each other when we must."[50]

[46] *Ibid.*
[47] Boston *Globe*, Dec. 22, 1898.
[48] *Ibid.*, Dec. 23.
[49] Brisbane to Bryan, Dec. 23, 1898, *Bryan Papers*, 27.
[50] Bryan to Carnegie, Dec. 24, 1898. *Bryan Papers*, 27. The italics are mine.

Bryan did not want to know how many Republicans would be arrayed against imperialism; he was confident—so he told Carnegie—that the majority of Democrats, Populists and free silver Republicans would oppose it and, at the same time, refuse to abandon the Chicago platform of 1896. "They cannot be tempted to surrender their convictions even by the hope of securing cooperation of those Republicans who see menace in Republican policies." As for himself, he would not want the presidency if he were unfree to carry out policies which he believed to be the need of the country. "I believe that the gold standard is a conspiracy against the human race," he insisted. And he concluded by observing that the lines of the next campaign could not be foreseen at this time. And to Brisbane he reiterated the same sentiment.[51]

Nor was this simply an effort to get out of what might prove an embarrassing position. His sincerity is clear from the fact that in the convention which nominated him in 1900, Bryan resolutely insisted, against great opposition, on a free silver plank, and only somewhat reluctantly consented to make imperialism the paramount issue.[52] Even making allowances for his unwillingness to admit that he had been in the wrong about free silver, one must recognize that Bryan was not desperately searching for an issue when he determined to urge the ratification of the treaty. He already had an issue. Bad as imperialism was, gold and trusts were worse, and he therefore refused to listen to Carnegie's pleas to abandon silver in order to concentrate with greater hope of success on imperialism. Besides, if he was not dishonest, he was hoping, as late as December 24, 1898, that this new question might be disposed of before the campaign of 1900.

Yet there is other evidence which indicates that Bryan's tactics were consciously determined by his political philosophy, and that he did intend to inject the issue of imperialism into the next political battle. That so great an issue as imperialism should be decided except by the people, was unthinkable. He was concerned not only with the end, but with the means. In spite of

[51] Bryan to Carnegie, Dec. 30, 1898; Bryan to Brisbane, Dec. 23, 1898.
[52] *Memoirs of William Jennings Bryan*, 125.

the fact that the majority of the people in 1896 decided for gold and McKinley, the people's champion had not lost faith in their ability rightly to decide a great political question, and he preferred to have the issue of imperialism submitted to them rather than to leave it to diplomacy or to another commission under the President. He had no desire to throw the matter back into the hands of the executive, and he urged that this would be the result if the treaty were rejected or amended.[53] Less than two weeks after Bryan told Carnegie that he was hoping that the question of imperialism might be disposed of before the campaign of 1900, he was writing to him in defense of his support of the treaty these significant words:

"Our cause is just, and I have faith in the people. . . . If the people are against us, a minority of the Senate cannot save us. . . . We ought not to succeed unless the people are with us."[54]

Confirmed in his belief that the treaty ought to be ratified, Bryan now also held that the whole issue should be submitted to the people. He did not suppose that they would again decide against him.

It is by no means clear why Bryan changed his position in the early days of January, 1899. Doubtless reasons of political expediency had some effect. Perhaps he saw that the sentiment against imperialism was growing. However that may have been, it is certain that his support of the treaty was also in part conditioned by the fact that he was realizing more clearly than ever before that he had no heart for the war, which, technically at least, had not yet come to an end.

The war, as a matter of fact, had crystallized the potential pacifism which had long been nourished by his Christian faith and his political and social philosophy, and which was, indeed, inherent in his personality. His experiences in the war had been unpleasant and unsuccessful in the bargain. He had learned that a war for a just principle, a holy war, might easily become a war of

[53] Bryan to Wilkinson Call, Jan. 12, 1899. *Bryan Papers.*
[54] Bryan to Carnegie, Jan. 13, 1899. *Bryan Papers, 27.*

conquest; that it might strengthen militarism and navalism, enrich the industrial and financial classes against which he had been struggling, and turn attention from the domestic problems he had close at heart. For such an outcome he would not take the responsibility—nor, if he could help it, would he let his party. In short, he turned against the war and all that was connected with it. Parents were clamoring for the return of their boys—he did not blame them. To a querulous mother he wrote that he favored the ratification of the treaty in order that the volunteers might be brought home.[55] Military expenditures were mounting. The President was, in December, 1898, recommending that the regular army be increased to 100,000 men, and Bryan insisted that this question must be met "now or not at all."[56] Trouble was brewing in the Philippines—on February 5, William Randolph Hearst suggested that the loss of twenty American lives at Manila was a reason for pushing the Treaty through the Senate more rapidly.[57] Bryan urged also that bloody insurrection could only be prevented by making immediate peace with Spain and accompanying that peace with a declaration of our purpose to grant the Filipinos their independence.[58] Other dangers, too, might arise if hostilities were prolonged. This point he had emphasized in his Savannah interview on December 14, and there were plenty of rumors in Washington to confirm it. England, Germany and Russia were, it was supposed, hostile to the spread of republicanism in the Orient—it threatened their empires. If we insisted that Spain recognize the Philippines as a republic, we might risk a conflict with the interests of European Powers. Rather than force Spain to give her rebellious archipelago its freedom, let the American people have that honor and glory. Bryan was, in short, convinced that it was better and easier to "persuade the American people to promise independence to the Filipinos in connection with the ratification of the treaty than to continue the war and force Spain to recognize a

[55] Bryan to Mrs. O. S. Wissler, Canton, Ohio, May 3, 1900, *Bryan Papers*, 14.
[56] Boston *Globe*, Dec. 24, and Dec. 15, 1898.
[57] Hearst to Bryan, Feb. 5, 1899. *Bryan Papers*, 27.
[58] Bryan to Hearst, *ibid*.

republic in the Philippines.[59]   In reality, there was no likelihood that Spain could continue the war,[60] or that the Powers would intervene; but Bryan believed that there was.   His opposition to war, although perhaps not the most important reason for his course, was a genuine one.

The result of Bryan's tactics was altogether different from his calculations.   In spite of his efforts, the Bacon resolution, which promised the Philippines their independence, failed by the vote of the Vice-President.   The administration thus won the treaty, with Bryan's aid; but in spite of his efforts, it defeated the Bacon resolution.   Had Bryan really desired above all else to inject the issue of imperialism into the campaign with any chance of success, he blundered badly indeed.   What he actually did was to crown McKinley's success, for the President could point to his victorious prosecution of the war and to its satisfactory conclusion.   Bryan thus "saved William McKinley from a defeat akin to that which befell Woodrow Wilson two decades later."[61]   Henry Cabot Lodge, trusting less in the people than the Great Commoner, did not hesitate to make use of a minority in the Senate to defeat the treaty of his political opponents.   Bryan was enough of a politician to defeat his anti-imperialistic and pacifistic desires.

Bryan's cup was indeed to be a bitter one.   Although he persuaded Senator William J. Stone to strengthen the anti-imperialistic position in the Democratic platform of 1900,[62] many in his party had been infected by the imperialistic virus and were discouraged by the substitution of anti-imperialism for free silver.[63] On the other hand, anti-imperialists, who supported Bryan once their plan for a third party fell through,[64] pleaded with the Demo-

[59] *Memoirs of William Jennings Bryan,* 121; *Speeches,* II, 21-22.

[60] Senator James K. Jones persuasively urged this point on Bryan.   Jones to Bryan, Jan. 24, 1899, *Bryan Papers,* 11.

[61] Charles and Mary Beard, *The Rise of American Civilization* (N. Y., 1927), II, 380.

[62] Bryan to Senator Wm. J. Stone, Lincoln, June 30, 1900, *Bryan Papers,* 24.

[63] *Memoirs of William Jennings Bryan,* 125.

[64] At the solicitation of Erving Winslow, promoter of the Anti-Imperialist League, Bryan elaborated satisfactorily in his acceptance speech at Indianapolis the anti-imperialist plank in the Democratic platform.

cratic candidate to abandon free silver completely in order to
defeat imperialism:

"Twice you have failed us (wrote David Starr Jordan). Once
when you justified the war with Spain, and once when you advised
the ratification of the Treaty of Peace with its infamous provisions,
in order to get rid of an issue which will not down. In both
cases, you felt no doubt that you were taking a choice of evils.
In the second case at least, you were surely in the wrong. . . .
today the strongest influence for imperialism is the silver agita-
tion. It threatens our tinsel prosperity, due we think, to the
beneficent wisdom of the President, and the people will have
none of it. If imperialism is an issue, it is the sole issue possible.
If you cannot make it so, it is your duty to stand aside for some
one else who can. . . . You have the chance to lead as Lincoln
and Sumner once led. Whether you win or lose, you have the
opportunity to place your name on the permanent roll of American
patriots, the glorious list of those who loved their country more
than party or power. Will you do this or shall we turn your
face to the wall, counting you only as one of the opportunists of
whom one is just as good as another?"[65]

Even some of the spokesmen of the peace movement, remembering Bryan's military title, wondered whether, if elected, he would
carry out his anti-imperialistic and anti-militaristic sentiments.[66]
The sweeping victory of Bryan's opponent provided no opportunity for such a test. How hopeless many of his supporters felt
is made clear in a letter from the most active representative of the
Anti-Imperialist League:

"It seems now as if the country was given over to carnage and
plunder—to blood and ashes. That there are a few thousands who
have not bowed the knee to Baal is slight consolation. The worst
of it all is that the American people have deliberately become partners in the great crimes we are committing, and have brutally
ordered that they be continued. Have not our "laboring men"
joyfully fitted their necks to the yoke? Is there any hope for such
a people?"[67]

[65] David Starr Jordan to Bryan, Stanford University, Feb. 7, 1900,
Bryan Papers, 27.
[66] *The Peacemaker,* 19, no. 5, Nov., 1900, 105. The *Advocate of Peace,*
(62, no. 8, Sept., 1900, 169) commended Bryan's acceptance speech at
Indianapolis.
[67] W. S. Croffut, Nov. 7, 1900, to Bryan, *Bryan Papers,* 13.

But Bryan kept his faith. Year after year his voice was heard trying to persuade the American people to repudiate imperialism. Through the chautauqua, in *The Commoner,* and in political campaigns he tried to show them the light. It was he who wrote into the Democratic platforms in 1904, 1908, and 1912 planks pledging his party to grant independence to the Philippines.[68] It was to him that Aguinaldo wrote in 1912 when a Democratic victory at last promised a new day, because he had always regarded Bryan as "the standard-bearer of justice, equality, and liberty."[69] Bryan's ideal was to become partially realized when, in the Wilson administration, the Jones Act became a law. And Bryan's ideal, extended to a larger stage, was the basis of Wilson's inspiring program of self-determination for all peoples.

Nor did Bryan during all these years keep silent regarding imperialism in other parts of the world. Both the Boers and the East Indians found in him a champion, and he did not hesitate to declare that while Great Britain had conferred benefits on India, the price exacted had been a terrible one.[70]

During the campaign of 1900 Bryan not only denounced imperialism but took occasion to make clear his growing opposition to navalism and to war, together with his confidence in the golden rule in international affairs. On receiving the platform from Senator William J. Stone, the Nebraska colonel took exception to the plank on the navy which, he feared, might be construed as support of "the imperialistic idea that our navy must be as large as any navy in the world." He went on to observe that "if we pursue a policy of justice and fair dealing, we do not need as

[68] Bryan to Wayne Williams, Jan. 26, 1923—*Bryan Papers,* 35. It is true that Bryan's speech at Manila in 1906 was disappointing to the Islanders. Bryan advised them to forego their demand for immediate independence, to support the government's plans for their advancement and progress, and to be patient. *The Commoner* insisted that Bryan's position had not materially changed—that he favored establishing a stable government, to be converted into a native one, and then to be made into a protectorate. *The Commoner,* 6, no. 13, May 18, 1906, and no. 5, Feb. 16, 1906.

[69] Aguinaldo to Bryan, Manila, Nov. 5, 1912, *Bryan Papers,* 36.

[70] Frederick Harrison, *Autobiographic Memories* (London, 1911), II, 206; W. A. Croffut to Bryan, Jan. 5, 1901, *Bryan Papers,* 14; William Jennings Bryan, *British Rule in India* (London, 1906).

big a navy as a land grabbing nation."[71] Bryan had his way:
the Kansas City platform made no mention of the navy, and the
plank denouncing militarism was all that any but the most doctrinaire pacifist could have desired.[72] In his speeches he pled for
peace. At Canton, Ohio, he spoke clearly:

"I hope that you will not merely, from the possession of that
cannon, be led to believe that war is a thing to be desired. It ought
to be further away from a Republic even than from a monarchy,
because in a monarchy the Government rests upon force. . . . I
believe that if this nation will stand upon its rights and be as
careful to respect the rights of other people as it is to defend its
own, there will be little use of war."[73]

America, he felt, was destined to be the arbiter of world disputes:

"Behold a republic increasing in population, in wealth, in strength,
and in influence, solving the problems of civilization and hastening
the coming of an universal brotherhood—a republic which makes
thrones and dissolves aristocracies by its silent example and gives
light and inspiration to those who sit in darkness. Behold a republic gradually but surely becoming the supreme moral factor in
disputes."[74]

This was an expression of the optimism and faith which kept
Bryan from despairing of his country. Instead of being disillu-
sioned on discovering that a war which had been, presumably,
fought in the cause of humanity had in reality brought imperialism,
Bryan became a pacifist. In no small part his pacifism was the
natural result of his early Christian training and his personality,
but it was also a compensation for the rapid victory of imperialism
and navalism, symbols of the new America.

This point of view and faith came to be confirmed and deepened as a result of the influence of Tolstoy, whom he visited at
Yasnaya Polyana in the winter of 1902-1903. This great apostle
of the doctrine of non-resistance acknowledged indebtedness to

[71] Bryan to Wm. J. Stone, Lincoln, June 30, 1900, *Bryan Papers*, 34.
[72] *Democratic Campaign Book, Presidential Election,* 1900 (Washington, 1900), 5-6.
[73] *The Peacemaker,* 19, no. 5, Nov., 1900, 105.
[74] William Jennings Bryan, *Speeches,* II, 49.

William Lloyd Garrison and to Adin Ballou, American exponents of that philosophy.[75]   Now, as it were, the process of cross-fertilization of ideas was further exemplified.   Tolstoy had indicted all war whatever as unnecessary murder, cruel, futile, and senseless.   Peace could be achieved, he taught, not through arbitration tribunals, but only through the refusal of men to support, in any way at all, war and preparation for war.   Tolstoy further insisted that love alone could conquer force and violence.   No war could be just, because force itself was an expression of the lowest animal passions in man—passions which could be checked by "inner exploration of self" and by rational observance of the divine law of love in every human relation.[76]

For several hours the young American—Bryan was only 42—discussed with the venerable Russian, whom he regarded as the moral Titan of Europe, the problem of war and peace, of violence and non-violence, of resistance and non-resistance.[77]   Bryan was not without doubts and questionings, but Tolstoy seems to have convinced him of an essential in his doctrine—the power of love. Tolstoy's report of the interview is much briefer than that of Bryan:

"A few days ago", wrote Tolstoy early in 1904, "I read in one of the leading magazines the opinion of an intelligent and clever writer that my recognition of the principle of non-resistance is a sad and partly comical error, which, taking into consideration my old age, and some of my deserts, one may pass with condescending silence.   Just such an attitude toward this question I met in my conversation with the remarkably clever and progressive American, Bryan.   He, also with apparent intention to show me my error in a gentle and respectful manner, asked me how I would explain my queer attitude as to non-resistance, and, as usual, brought forth the seemingly uncontradictable argument about the murderer, who before my eyes kills or outrages a child.   I told him that I uphold non-resistance, because, having lived seventy-five years I

[75] Fanny Garrison Villard, *William Lloyd Garrison on Non-Resistance*, (New York, 1924) "What I Owe to Garrison"—a letter from Tolstoy to V. Tchertkoff, Jan., 1904, 46 ff.

[73] Count Leo Tolstoy, "Bethink Yourselves", *The Living Age*, 242 (1904), 257-261.

[77] William Jennings Bryan, *Under Other Flags* (Lincoln, 1905) 96 ff.; Bryan, *The Old World and Its Ways*, (St. Louis, 1907), 561.

have never except in conversations, met that fantastic murderer who before my eyes wanted to kill or outrage a child, but I have constantly seen not one, but a million murderers outraging children and women and adults, old men and old women, and all working people, in the name of the permitted right of violence over their equals. When I said this my kind interlocutor, with his peculiar quickness of perception, did not give me a chance to finish, but began to laugh and found my argument satisfactory."[78]

He probably over-stated this last point. Although Bryan regarded his visit to the great Russian as the most satisfactory of his European experiences, hung a picture of him in his home, read and quoted from his writings, and maintained some contact through correspondence with him,[79] he did not accept outright the entire Tolstoyan philosophy. What impressed him most of all was Tolstoy's conviction that love was a more powerful force than brute violence—that it was, in short, both shield and armor. Tolstoy taught him that the sway of the heart not only bound all men together—he had always believed this—but that it also ruled the world. In speech after speech Bryan showed the influence of Tolstoy. Attacking Roosevelt in 1904 as an exponent of force, Bryan took him to task for eulogizing war and for declaring that the era of perpetual peace would never come.

"This is an exalting of the doctrine of brute force; it darkens the hopes of the race. . . . If this is the doctrine that our nation is to stand for, it is retrogression, not progress. *It is a turning backward to the age of violence.* More than that, it is nothing less than a challenge to the Christian civilization of the world."[80]

Appeal to conscience was the dominant note in a speech on "Peace" delivered to the Holland Society in January, 1904.[81] Two

---

[78] *The Independent,* 56, Apr. 21, 1904, 882.
[79] *Memoirs of William Jennings Bryan,* 460-461; *World Peace Foundation Pamphlets,* 1912, no. 7, Pt. II, 11-12; *The Old World and its Ways,* 563. Bryan, in his audience with the czar, congratulated him on his work for arbitration at The Hague. But it is clear that he was far more impressed by Tolstoyism as a means to peace. Bryan in 1904 was also influenced towards non-resistance by reading a letter of Dumas. See "The Forces that Make for Peace", *loc. cit.,* 167.
[80] *Speeches,* II, 51-52.
[81] *Under Other Flags,* 293 ff.

years later, in speaking to the parliamentarians at their international conference in London, Bryan thought it was not too much to hope that the day might be hastened "when we shall feel so appalled at the thought of the taking of any human life that we shall strive to raise all questions to a level where the settlement will be by reason and not by force."[82] The indissoluble bonds which unite each human being to every other, he went on to say, were the only foundation on which permanent peace could be built. At about the same time he went even further in expressing, in a press interview, a fundamental conception of Tolstoy's:

"But, of course, permanent peace must be founded in justice, and justice is impossible without the full recognition of our relations and duties to others and the full performance of them. This depends upon a realization of the brotherhood of man, an appreciation of the value of love as life, the prevalence of love among the people of all countries. Permanent peace and justice depend upon the manifestation of love in all hearts, so that we would be horrified at the thought of the taking of life by the people of one country at war with the people of another."[83]

In his reception speech in New York in 1906 Bryan confessed that his aversion to the taking of life had increased with the years.[84] More and more he acknowledged Tolstoy's leadership:

"I suppose", he told an audience in 1910, "that the most significant example in all this world today of one who lives as he preaches this doctrine of love is the case of Tolstoy. He is not only a believer in the doctrine of love, but he is a believer in the doctrine of non-resistance, and there he stands proclaiming to the world that he believes that love is a better protection than force; that he thinks a man will suffer less by refusing to use violence than if he used it. And what is the result: He is the only man in Russia that the czar with all his army dare not lay his hand on. . . . The power that is about him, the power that is over him and the power that is in him is proof against violence. I believe it would be true of a nation. I believe that this nation could stand before the world today and tell the world that it did not believe in war, that it did not believe that it was the right way to settle disputes, that it had no disputes that it was not willing to submit to the judgment of the

[82] *Speeches*, II.
[83] *Independent*, "The Path to Peace", 61, (1906), 487.
[84] *Speeches*, II, 66.

world. If this nation did that, it not only would not be attacked by any other nation on earth, but it would become the supreme power in the world. I have no doubt of it, and I believe that the whole tendency is toward that policy."[85]

Further than this Bryan did not go: but he did insist that there existed no question today, nor could exist any question tomorrow, which Christ's gospel of love and brotherhood could not solve.[86] Nowhere did he give evidence that he accepted Tolstoy's doctrine of anarchistic opposition on the part of the individual to what he regarded as morally unjustifiable behavior on the part of the state. Bryan's political faith in the people, and their agent, the state, kept him from subscribing to the doctrine of war resistance. The spirit of the conscientious objector he never entertained or even understood. Indeed, Bryan thought that Tolstoy in condemning church and state failed to appreciate the great aid which organization, political and religious, could lend when properly directed.[87]

Bryan's travels in Europe and in the Orient, his contact with foreign statesmen and foreign peoples, greatly widened his outlook and deepened his conviction that the human heart everywhere is the same; that all men are truly brothers; and that it should be the function of the United States to hasten the realization of that cardinal truth. True, his foreign experience as reflected in his platitudinous speeches did not give him any very realistic insight into the complicated social, political, economic and psychological causes of war; but it is an exaggeration to say, as one of his biographers has said, that the Peerless Leader believed that so long as he could treat the world to a big smile, the affairs of the world would right themselves.[88] He was not too simple to see, especially in his later years, that war resulted from complex

[85] "The Forces that Make for Peace," *loc. cit.,* 172. The fullest statement which Bryan made of this position was at Edinburgh, in "An Address delivered at the World's Missionary Conference, June 17, 1910," in *The Fruits of the Tree,* (London and Edinburgh, 1910).

[86] Bryan, *Fruits of the Tree,* 38-39.

[87] Bryan, *Under Other Flags,* 102 ff.

[88] M. R. Werner, *Bryan* (N. Y., 1929), 145 ff.

forces—race hatreds, propaganda, and, above all, the profit motive, which might express itself in commercial rivalry or in the ambitions of munition makers. War, he once remarked, was a boil which indicated that there was poison in the blood.[89]

During the first decade of the new century Bryan identified himself increasingly with the peace movement which he interpreted as "an outgrowth, a symptom, an illustration" of the awakening sense of brotherhood. True, he hardly thought it necessary to accept Captain R. P. Hobson's challenge to debate the issue of navalism, inasmuch as the Democratic party had, in its national convention of 1904, unanimously accepted a plank condemning Hobson's idea of the paramount need for a great navy.[90] Yet again and again in popular speeches he attacked the idea that a large navy was the best guarantee of peace, and he condemned the use of the navy for the collection of debts.[91]

"I believe that our nation can take a long step in advance now", he said in 1910, "by announcing . . . that the navy will not be used for the collection of debts; that as we do not imprison people for debt in this country, we will not man battleships and kill people because they owe people in this country; that we will apply to international affairs the very doctrines we apply to our national affairs, and if any one in the United States wishes to invest money in another country he must do so according to the laws of that country. Then every nation would be open to American investments. For that is the kind of investments they would look for. They have had enough of investments which are preceded by the purchase of a little land to be followed by a battleship that takes the rest of the country."

This sounds very much like Wilson's denunciation of dollar diplomacy in his Mobile speech in 1913.[92] With such arguments, together with an insistence that patriotism and profits were often intermingled in the demand for a greater navy,[93] Bryan struck at the Hobsons and the Mahans and the Roosevelts.

[89] William Jennings Bryan, *In His Image* (N. Y., 1922), 233.
[90] Bryan to Captain R. P. Hobson, Mar. 27, 1905, *Bryan Papers*, 27.
[91] "The Forces that Make for Peace," *loc. cit.*, 172.
[92] Ray Stannard Baker and William E. Dodd, *The Public Papers of Woodrow Wilson*, (N. Y., 1926), I, 64 ff, "A New Latin-American Policy."
[93] William Jennings Bryan, "The Forces that Make for Peace", *loc. cit.*, 171.

With increasing frequency this advocate of peace was to be found at arbitration meetings and anti-war organizations, in Great Britain as well as in America, developing his philosophy of love as the basis of international relations and human brotherhood, and the golden rule as the path to peace.[94] Specifically, he contributed to the peace movement's program, not only through his advocacy of his treaty plan, but also by championing the principle that neutrals should not lend money to belligerents,[95] and that no war should be declared, except in case of actual invasion, without a referendum of the people.

Bryan's message of peace, however, reached far more people through his weekly, *The Commoner,* and through his speeches at the chautauquas, than it did through the peace congresses which he addressed. One of the earliest of the chautauqua lecturers, he remained the most popular one for thirty years. How many people he reached through this means cannot even be estimated, but they must have numbered millions. Before the era of the automobile, whole families migrated to town from the surrounding farms, after the wheat was harvested, for chautauqua. Often they brought with them provisions and tents, and refreshed themselves from weary toil and monotonous routine. Under the scorching canvas of the big tent tired women in calico, gingham and sunbonnets fanned themselves interminably and nursed their babies; tall gaunt men, failures and half-failures, took in part of what Bryan said, at least; self-conscious youths and even children heard

[94] The most notable of Bryan's addresses before peace societies were "Peace", delivered in June, 1904 (*Under Other Flags,* 301 ff.) ; Address at the London conference of the Inter-parliamentary Union (*Speeches,* II, 226 ff ; Address at the National Arbitration and Peace Congress in New York, 1907 (*Proceedings of,* 85, 312 ff.) ; "The Forces that Make for Peace," *Report of the Sixteenth Annual Meeting of the Lake Mohonk Conference on International Arbitration,* May, 1910, 164 ff.

[95] This was not a new idea. War loans had been condemned at every universal peace congress since the one held in Paris in 1849. The first specific application of the idea to neutrals seems to have been in 1894 at Antwerp, when the Congress condemned loans by European and American neutrals to China and Japan. *Resolutions Textuelles des Congres Universels de la Paix tenus de 1843 à 1910* (Berne, 1912), 76-77. For Bryan's position on this point see *The National Peace and Arbitration Congress,* (N. Y., 1907), 313.

the melodious cadences of Bryan's voice. Fortified against the heat by a pitcher of ice water, the great orator with happy humor and no end of anecdotes, exalted and uplifted his rural audiences.[96] Many of them heard from him for the first time the application of their own religious feelings to the problem of war and peace in words that profoundly moved them.[97] As a popularizer of the ideal of human brotherhood, Bryan was indeed the Peerless Leader. What his influence was on these people, who can say, what his contribution to a growing peace consciousness, who can be sure? Perhaps his greatest contribution to the peace movement lay in these chautauqua lectures—this is one of the imponderables. Yet it can fairly be said that, unmeasurable though this contribution is, it was certainly a positive one: and it mitigates, how much or how little cannot be said, the seeming futility of his long and arduous battle against the war system. But before explaining why it was so futile, it is necessary to evaluate his specific and concrete labors to objectify and realize the philosophy of peace to which he had come gradually but surely.

[96] Some of the chautauqua lectures in which the peace message was emphasized were "A Conquering Nation" (*Under Other Flags,* 247 ff.) ; "The Value of an Ideal", *ibid.,* 242; and "The Prince of Peace."
[97] This description is suggested by that of Helen Edith Marshall, *The Social Philosophy of William Jennings Bryan* (Master's Thesis, University of Chicago.)

II

THE THIRTY TREATIES

Eight years before Bryan became secretary of state he elaborated the plan which remains his most important contribution to the peace movement. Early in 1905 he suggested that the United States ought to take the initiative in framing a system of arbitration so comprehensive that *all* differences would be submitted to a commission or an arbitration court. Up to this time, no important public man had ventured to suggest that *every* sort of dispute, even those involving national honor and vital interest, should be referred to arbitration or conciliation. Bryan, it is true, hastened to add that each nation would reserve the right to reject the findings of arbitration if it believed them incompatible with its honor or integrity.[1] Somewhat later he urged President Roosevelt to negotiate treaties by which "any and every international dispute" be submitted to the Hague court for investigation.[2] On October 20, 1905, he presented his idea, in a more concrete form, to a group of Japanese statesmen:[3] every dispute was to be submitted to a permanent tribunal for investigation; there was to be no resort to war until a report and recommendation had been made; and the parties were to be free to act only after the report had been published. True to his philosophy of peace, he included in his scheme no provision for compulsion or the enforced carrying out of the recommendations of the commission. He believed that the period of delay and the force of public opinion were in themselves sufficient to make war extremely unlikely, and that nations would, on second sober thought, voluntarily accept the findings of the investigation and do what was right and just.

---

[1] *The Commoner,* Feb. 17, 1905. Bryan in 1915 said that this editorial in *The Commoner* was, so far as he could recall, the first suggestion of his peace plans. Bryan to Harry Walker, Jan. 20, 1915, *Misc. correspondence, 1913-25,* 28.

[2] *Ibid.,* Feb. 17, 24, 1905; Sept. 15, 1905.

[3] *Memoirs,* 385. According to Bryan, the response was not very encouraging.

If this seemed Utopian, it was entirely in accord with the philosophy of love and the golden rule which he had made his own.

This program was, indeed, no more original than Bryan's philosophy of peace itself. As early as 1870 a proposal had been made in the National Association for the Promotion of Social Science for an international code requiring nations to give six months notice before going to war.[4] Four years later the American jurist, David Dudley Field, suggested in his "Project for an International Code" an arrangement by which, before resort to war, disputes of every sort were to be submitted to a commission, and if that failed to bring adjustment, to an arbitral tribunal.[5] That same year petitions were circulated[6] asking the President and Congress "to seek an express stipulation between nations, that they will not resort to war till peaceful arbitration has been tried, and never without a full year's previous notice." In both these suggestions emphasis was placed on the importance of a period of delay for the cooling of national passions. The Universal Peace Congress in London in 1890 had also taken the position that the most dangerous wars would be avoided if a delay could be obtained during which passion might be appeased. This congress recommended, therefore, the establishment of juridical tribunals, independent of the executive power, for the examination of all disputes which threatened conflict. It was perhaps this action which led William Blymyer, of Mansfield, Ohio, to propose in 1892 a ten-year treaty by which all disputes were to be referred to commissions of investigation.[7] Finally, the First Hague Convention had recommended international commissions of inquiry to facilitate a solution of disputes "by elucidating the facts by means of an impartial and conscientious investigation." True, this was a mere recommendation. The commissions of inquiry

[4] *Sessional proceedings of the National Association for the Promotion of Social Science for the year* 1870-1871, IV, 17-18.
[5] Henry M. Field, *The Life of David Dudley Field* (N. Y., 1898), 234-235.
[6] *Advocate of Peace*, n.s., V, Jan., 1874, 1.
[7] *Résolutions textuelles des congres universels de la paix* (Berne, 1912), 35-36; *The Peacemaker*, XI, no. 7, Jan., 1893, 126.

were not, as in the Bryan plan, to be permanent, and their function was to be limited to an investigation of "differences of opinion on points of fact."[8] Still, it can fairly be said that the essential elements of Bryan's peace plan had all been proposed before he first outlined his program in 1905. He was apparently unaware of all these suggestions and facts, and came to his idea independently. It was, in fact, the existence of commissions of inquiry in disputes between capital and labor that suggested to him the extension of the idea to the sphere of international relations.[9] Thus the practical politician who was to put into effect ideas previously elaborated by the peace movement, would quite likely have come to those ideas had that movement never sponsored such a program.

The very year after Bryan first proposed his peace plan in *The Commoner,* good fortune enabled him to present it to the Interparliamentary Union, an organization made up of members of legislative bodies meeting annually for the promotion of arbitration and international peace.[10] While in Norway, he received an invitation from Lord Weardale to attend the conference of the Interparliamentary Union in London in July, 1906. Lord Weardale and Sir Henry Campbell-Bannerman, the premier, heard Bryan explain his plan, and endorsed it.[11] Already the Interparliamentary Union had been favorably prepared for considering the plan by reason of the work of another American, Richard Bartholdt. This Republican congressman from St. Louis, who founded the American group of the Interparliamentary Union and

[8] At the Second Hague Conference the Powers, armed to the teeth and anxious to lose no advantage, rejected a plan for a delay of twenty-four hours between an ultimatum and the outbreak of hostilities in order to give time for a peaceful settlement of the dispute. What that conference was unable to do, Bryan substantially accomplished by his thirty treaties— and far more. James Brown Scott, "Remarks at the American Society of International Law, April 26, 1929", typewritten report.

[9] *Memoirs of William Jennings Bryan,* 384. Bryan had for many years been advocating investigation in labor disputes. Bryan to Wayne Williams, Jan. 26, 1923, *Bryan Papers,* 35.

[10] *The Inter-Parliamentary Union, Its Work and Organization.* 3 ed. (Geneva, 1930).

[11] *Memoirs of William Jennings Bryan,* 385.

brought the parliamentarians to America for their meeting in 1904,[12] had independently presented in his draft treaty of 1905 the main idea of Bryan's proposal.[13] Bartholdt's "General Treaty of Arbitration," considerably amended by the special committee appointed for its consideration, was laid before the London conference of the Interparliamentary Union. Bryan moved an amendment to the document in these words:

"If a disagreement should occur between the contracting parties which, in the terms of the arbitration treaty, need not be submitted to arbitration, they shall, before declaring war or engaging in any hostilities, submit the question in controversy to the Hague Court or some other impartial international tribunal for investigation and report, each party reserving the right to act independently afterwards."[14]

In a well received speech before the Conference,[15] Bryan explained his idea. His resolution, he said, was in harmony with the arbitration treaty under consideration, and more important even than the treaty itself. Certain questions affecting the honor and integrity of a nation were considered outside the jurisdiction of a court of arbitration, but it was just these questions which made the most trouble. Passion was seldom aroused by minor questions which were held to be arbitrable; but arbitration was often not employed even in such questions for fear that they might involve larger issues of national integrity and national honor. Then he succinctly stated the advantages of his plan:

"The first advantage, then, of this resolution is that it secures an investigation of the facts, and if you can but separate the facts from the question of honour, the chances are 100 to 1 that you can settle both the fact and the question of honour without war. There is, therefore, a great advantage in an investigation which brings out

[12] Richard Bartholdt, *From Steerage to Congress* (Phil., 1930), XVI-XVII. The parliamentary visitors were deeply touched by an address on the question of peace which Bryan made to them while they were on a tour of Colorado. Bartholdt, *op. cit.,* 204. Bryan's speech is printed in *Tour of the Interparliamentary Union in the United States,* 1904.

[13] *Union Interparlementaire XIII e Conference* (Bruxelles, 1905), 154; Chr. Lange, *The American Peace Treaties* (Kristiania, 1915), 8.

[14] *Official Report of the XIV Conference* (London, 1907), 116-121.

[15] William Jennings Bryan, *Speeches,* II, 226 ff.

the facts; for disputed facts between nations, as between friends, are the cause of most disagreements. (Cheers).

"The second advantage of this investigation is that it gives time for calm consideration. I need not say to you that man excited is a very different animal from man calm, and that questions ought to be settled, not by passion, but by deliberation. If this resolution would do nothing else but give time for reflection and deliberation, there would be sufficient reason for its adoption. If we can but stay the hand of war until conscience can assert itself, war will be made more remote. When men are mad they swagger around and tell what they can do; when they are calm they consider what they ought to do. (Cheers).

"The third advantage of this investigation is that it gives opportunity to mobilize public opinion for the compelling of a peaceful settlement, and that is an advantage not to be overlooked. Public opinion is coming to be more and more a power in the world. . . ."[16]

After Bryan's resolution had been discussed by the Interparliamentary Council, it was submitted, with some amendments, to the full conference, and approved as an alternative to mediation. Particularly noteworthy is the amendment by which recourse to "the Hague Court or some other impartial international tribunal for investigation and report" was changed to read "to an International Commission of Inquiry" or to mediation. By this amendment a clear line was drawn "between the functions of a tribunal and those of a body of investigation and conciliation."[17] Without opposition the conference accepted the amended Bryan resolution. This was the first official recognition of his peace plan.

Bryan's success at the London Interparliamentary Conference not only gave official status to his project; it also made him a recognized leader in the international peace movement. Lord Bryce reported that he had made a favorable impression in London, and that his speech was "certainly splendid."[18] Sir Randal Cremer, veteran leader of the workingman's peace movement, regarded his address as "one of the most expressive and striking

[16] *Ibid.*
[17] Chr. L. Lange, *The American Peace Treaties* (Kristiania, 1915), 8.
[18] M. A. DeWolf Howe, *James Ford Rhodes.* (N. Y., 1929), 136.

pleas for international arbitration, applied to all subjects of international agreement", that he had ever heard, and felt that his success in getting the approval of the Interparliamentary Conference
for his plan was an "event of enormous significance."   At a
luncheon which Campbell-Bannerman arranged, the lord high chancellor, Lord Loreburn, congratulated the Nebraskan on his speech.
Whitelaw Reid presented him to King Edward, with whom he discussed arbitration and peace; and he was besieged by callers.[19]
During a dinner given him by Haldane he encouraged the latter
to work for a limitation of armaments.   Almost all the London
papers printed his speech, many commenting favorably on it.   The
Daily Express called it "terse, rapid, epigrammatical"; the London
Times, which fifty years before scornfully belittled similar talk
about peace, observed that the force and fire of such an appeal,
by becoming translated into the actual, was not lost.   The *Daily
Mail* commended his eloquence, and such journals as the *West-
minster Gazette* and the *Evening Standard* and *St. James Gazette*
were enthusiastic.[20]   This indeed was Bryan's day.   His success
irritated some of his American foes: the Kansas City *Republican*
complained that the "hero of the hour" had never given any time
or serious thought to the great cause of peace.[21]   But in spite of
such querulous attacks, Bryan's prestige at home was enhanced by
the recognition he had won from foreign parliamentarians and
statesmen.

Having won the ear of the world for his plan, Bryan lost no
opportunity for presenting it in and out of season.   The Lake
Mohonk conference on arbitration heard him discuss it; so did the
National Peace and Arbitration Congress in New York in 1907;
so did chautauqua audiences.   The Interparliamentary Union endorsed the principle at subsequent meetings.[22]

Bryan's idea found its way partially into the arbitration treaties

[19] *The Commoner,* VI, Aug. 3, 1906, 8 ff; Campbell-Bannermann to
Bryan, July 9, 1906, *Bryan Papers,* 36.
[20] *The Commoner,* July 20, 1906, 12; Aug. 17, 1906, 4 ff.
[21] *The Commoner,* VI, Aug. 3, 1906.
[22] William Jennings Bryan, *Speeches,* II, 65; *Proceedings of the Arbitration and Peace Congress* (N. Y., 1907), 313, 298.

which Taft and Knox negotiated in 1911 with Great Britain and France. On June 29, 1910, Bryan, having presented his plan to an Edinburgh meeting, wrote a persuasive letter to Taft. He told the President that he had learned from cabinet members that the British government would probably consent to a treaty based on his plan, and urged Taft to take the initiative.[23] After negotiations for arbitration treaties had been begun, Bryan visited the White House, and the President, pleased with the suggestion of embodying the Commoner's ideas in the treaties, called in the Secretary of State, Knox, who likewise expressed approval. Then Bryan presented his plan to the British ambassador, Lord Bryce.[24] When the treaties were drawn up, it was plain that they borrowed much from the Bryan plan. Although treaties of arbitration, they were intended "to provide means for the peaceful solution of all questions of difference which it shall be found impossible in the future to settle by diplomacy." This was a recognition of one of the essential ideas that Bryan had emphasized. The second article in the text provided for the creation of joint high commissions of inquiry, instituted for each difference, and committing the parties to abstain from hostilities during the year in which the commission made its investigation. Like the Bryan proposal, the recommendations of the commission were not to be binding.[25] Although the Senate approved of this aspect of the treaties, they were emasculated by amendments reserving to itself the decision, in each particular instance, of submitting or not submitting disputes to arbitration or investigation. Taft in the end abandoned the treaties rather than accept the amendments. He did, however, give Bryan credit for his contribution.[26] Thus the Bryan idea made checkered headway.

[23] Bryan to Taft, June 29, 1910, *Bryan Papers*, 27.

[24] *Memoirs of William Jennings Bryan*, 385; *The Commoner*, 14, Sept., 1914, 3. For Taft's high opinion of Bryan at about this time see Archibald Wellington Butt, *Taft and Roosevelt. The Intimate Letters of Archie Butt* (N. Y., 1930) I, 286, 330.

[25] *World Peace Foundation Pamphlets* (Boston, 1916), VI, no. 5, 19-21; Chr. L. Lange, *The American Peace Treaties*, 10; *The Commoner*, 14, Sept., 1914, 3; *Memoirs of William Jennings Bryan*, 385.

[26] William Howard Taft, *The United States and World Peace* (N. Y., 1914), 131.

No wonder that the peace movement rejoiced when Bryan became secretary of state in March, 1913.[27] At the very time that he assumed the responsibilities of this office, he publicly declared that he could never take part in any negotiations which would lead his country into any kind of a foreign war.[28] When had anyone vested with the direction of the foreign affairs of a major Power ever made such a commitment?

Moreover, not a month had passed before friends of peace learned that he had taken carefully planned steps for the negotiation of treaties embodying his program. When the President elect had invited him to Princeton and offered him the first place in the cabinet, the peace leader had secured Wilson's approval for the cause so close to his heart. As a result of cabinet discussion, certain minor changes were made in the draft which Bryan had drawn up. Determined not to encounter the hostility of the Senate, he went to its committee on foreign affairs and won its approval. Then, on April 24, 1913, he summoned the diplomatic corps and proposed the negotiation of treaties committing the parties to submit all questions, without exception, to an investigating commission, and to abstain from hostilities until the commission's report had been made.[29] The commissions, appointed prior to the dispute and permanent in personnel, were to be composed of one subject or citizen from each nation, chosen by that nation, and one chosen by each nation from a foreign state, with a fifth commissioner to be selected by agreement of the two contracting parties. The right to act independently, after the commission had reported, was clearly stipulated. Partly owing to the objection of the Senate committee on foreign affairs, and partly to fear that the larger foreign Powers might oppose, a provision that the period of investigation should not be used for a change

---

[27] *Advocate of Peace*, LXXV, Apr., 1913, 73, July, 1913, 146-7.

[28] Albert Shaw, "William Jennings Bryan", *Review of Reviews*, 72, Aug., 1925, 260; Josephus Daniels, "Wilson and Bryan," *Saturday Evening Post*, Sept. 5, 1925, 54 ff.

[29] Statement made by Bryan, April 24, 1913, to the thirty-six representatives of foreign nations at Washington. *Foreign Relations of the United States*, 1913, 8-11.

in the naval or military program of the contracting parties, was omitted.[30] The diplomats expressed their approval, and Bryan, after waiting for them to consult their governments, took up with each the negotiation of a separate treaty along the lines laid down. These treaties differed in detail, although they were alike in their main features. Had an effort been made to achieve absolute uniformity, probably no treaty would have been signed at all. Concessions in the matter of phraseology smoothed away many a rough place in the negotiations; and Bryan wisely did not wait for all the governments to agree. He dealt, rather, with each separately.[31]

On August 17, 1913, the first treaty was signed, with Salvador; the Netherlands was the first European country to come into the arrangement. Altogether thirty treaties were negotiated, and twenty ratifications exchanged. Bryan showed much greater skill in handling the senate than his predecessors: he submitted a statement in advance to the committee on foreign affairs, setting forth the interpretation that all disputed questions could be submitted directly to international commissions without previous consent of the senate.[32] When twenty-seven nations had committed themselves to the plan, Bryan, in high spirits, celebrated the event by distributing to the respective diplomats souvenirs in the form of a paperweight representing a plowshare beaten out of an obsolete army sword provided by the war department.[33] He took great pride in his achievement, and even after the world war broke out, pursued his course without any less energy or, so far as could be seen, any less optimism. He regarded this as his greatest contribution to world peace.

The organized peace movement welcomed the Bryan treaties with enthusiasm, urged governments to ratify them, and did its

---

[30] *Bryan Papers, Correspondence,* 1913-1925, copy of the peace plan submitted to the President early in April, with memoranda. New York *Times,* Apr. 24, Apr. 27, 1913.

[31] *The Commoner,* 14, Aug., 1914, 6-7.

[32] Bryan to Sir Cecil Spring-Rice, Aug. 24, 1914, *Bryan Papers,* 36; and Bryan to Sir Cecil Spring-Rice, June 30, 1914. The Senate ratified the treaties with little or no opposition.

[33] Stephen Gwynn, *The Letters and Friendships of Sir Cecil Spring-Rice,* (London, 1929), II, 240; *Advocate of Peace,* LXXVI, Dec., 1914, 256.

best to popularize their principles.[34]   In this activity it was supported by other international groups such as the Freemasons[35] and some religious bodies.   The Interparliamentary Union warmly recommended the plan to official authorities, and distinguished publicists pointed out the merits of the Bryan idea.   The permanency of the commissions was praised, the inclusion of questions of national honor and vital interest, excluded in previous treaties, was heartily commended.   Dr. Christian Lange noted that the treaties introduced a new procedure, that of elucidation and investigation *before* either mediation or conciliation.[36]   A leading Dutch pacifist praised Bryan for greatly extending the principle of international commissions by making them mediators as well as fact-finders.[37]   Prior to the outbreak of the war, the general response of internationalists was favorable, although the most constructive and penetrating criticism came from avowed friends of peace rather than from skeptics and scoffers.   Once the war had broken out, many pacifists tried to find some consolation in the Bryan movement.[38]

While the courageous German pacifist, Alfred Fried, rejoiced that political conflicts were to be divested of their inflammable qualities by making the principle of postponement an integral part of international law,[39] another veteran leader of the German peace movement, Pastor Umfrid, was less optimistic.[40]   Finding much in the treaties to commend, he felt, none the less, that they were essentially superficial in that they neglected the idea of inter-

[34] In sending Bryan a copy of his *War Abolished*, Carnegie added a postscript: "to William Jennings Bryan, a notable champion of peace, foremost negotiator of international peace treaties which insure to nations a whole year for peaceful negotiation which is certain to result in the triumph of peace ninety-nine times out of a hundred." *Memoirs of William Jennings Bryan*, 388.   Another pacifist, Dr. David Starr Jordan, promised Bryan to popularize the principles of his peace plan during a world tour.   New York *Times*, Oct. 24, 1914.

[35] James Richardson to Bryan, Dec. 5, 1915, *Misc. Letters*, 1914-1923.

[36] Lange, *The American Peace Treaties*, 14-15, 63.

[37] *La Paix par le Droit*, 24 anné, 10 Juin, 1914, 330 ff.

[38] *The Arbitrator*, Oct., 1914, 112; *Concord*, July-August, 1915, 197; *Herald of Peace*, Oct., 1914, 105.

[39] *The Commoner*, 14, Mar. 1914, 15 ff.

[40] *Volker-Friede*, 14 Jahrgang, Nov., 1913, 113-115.

national federation, which, he thought, could alone prevent war. Norman Angell ignored the fact-finding emphasis of the Bryan plan, going so far as to declare that Bryan's good intention and sentimental declarations probably was costing the peace movement tragic failure.[41] In France, the well-known legal scholar and peace advocate, Jacques Dumas, pointed out practical difficulties.[42] If all the states made treaties with all other states, he urged, there would be 1806 commissions, and this might be somewhat confusing! In case of a dispute between one government and two or three others, just which commission would function? Others realized that certain categories of disputes involved far too complex issues, emotions and prejudices for investigation by a commission, disputes which even a year's delay could not prevent from festering into war. Even if the facts could be agreed upon, each disputant might still insist on the correctness of its own interpretation of the facts. With nationalism what it was, could one be at all certain that governments would voluntarily submit to a postponement of hostilities during an investigation, or accept the findings of the commission? These were some of the queries raised by the pacifists whose enemies supposed them to be impractical and vaguely idealistic.

Outside the circle of the peace movement, the Bryan treaties were not taken so seriously, partly because Bryan sponsored them, partly because they provided no sanctions, partly because the majority of them were signed after the world war had already defied the sanctity of international agreements. On April 27, 1913, the New York *Times* remarked that the Bryan treaties could not do any harm, and might do some good. Later, when treaties with some of the great Powers had been signed, the *Times* regarded them as a "splendid and solid contribution to the welfare of the world." It rose valiantly to their defence when Roosevelt attacked them on the ground that no nation, including our own, would pay the slightest attention to them in the event they were invoked in any matter where important interests were seriously

[41] *War and Peace*, I, May 8, 1914.
[42] *La Paix par le Droit*, 25 mars, 1914, 24 anné, 162-170.

154   SMITH COLLEGE STUDIES IN HISTORY

involved.[43]   But with some justice their author complained that they were given, in comparison with war news, a pitifully obscure place in the press.

In England, press comment was divided.   The London *Times* thought that the treaties marked no progress at all.   Pointing out that they did not provide for arbitration, but for mere investigation, the *Times* insisted that the treaties actually belonged to the period before the first Hague Conference, and arose merely from the reluctance of the American senate to allow any decision to pass out of its own power.[44]   Other British newspapers, particularly when it became clear that the administration attached so much seriousness to the treaties, were more favorable.   The London *Evening Standard* and the London *Review* urged the government to coöperate with the United States in the matter of the treaties, and after the repeal of the Panama Canal Tolls Exemption Act in July, 1914, British press opinion was distinctly favorable.[45]   Even the *Times* came to regard the treaties as "eminently practical."[46]

The French press, if represented at all by *Le Matin,* was caustic, dubbing Bryan a poet whom not even Plato would have in his Republic.[47]   The New York *Times* noted, early in February, 1914, an inclination on the part of the German press to be scornful towards Bryan's efforts.[48]   Taken altogether, the treaties seem to have had, at best, only a moderately good press.

Public officials took equally varying views.   Wilson spoke of the treaties as a means of "shedding light" on disputes as a result of which force would become obsolete.[49]   Later he maintained that if there could have been a delay of nine months on the eve of the world war, that catastrophe would have been prevented.[50] Franklin K. Lane testified that "we of America" did not take

[43] New York *Times,* Apr. 27, 1913, Sept. 17, Sept. 20, Oct. 4, 1914.
[44] *Herald of Peace,* no. 749, Oct., 1914, 105.
[45] New York *Times,* July 10, 1914.
[46] London *Times,* Sept. 28, 1914.
[47] Quoted by the New York *Times,* May 13, 1913.
[48] *Ibid.,* Feb. 16, 1914.
[49] *Ibid.,* Oct. 25, 1914.
[50] Speech at Indianapolis, New York *Times,* Sept. 5, 1919.

Bryan's treaties seriously, and yet he wrote their author that he would have his "place in history" for his contribution to the peace of the world.[51] Other cabinet members, so far as their published memoirs permit one to judge, did not regard the Bryan treaties as of much importance. Outside the cabinet, a few men whose word carried weight testified in their favor. Senator Burton endorsed the treaty plan before European law-makers and in the *Saturday Evening Post*,[52] and in 1921 declared that Bryan's work in this connection was "the most telling and valuable in the impetus towards world-wide peace, of the century".[53] Another advocate of peace, Hon. George Gray, a distinguished jurist, thought that no one in public life had done so much for the practical promotion of the cause of peace.[54] Senator Norris found it impossible to imagine how there could be war between any two nations observing the terms of these treaties.[55] Against such judgments must be placed that of Roosevelt who, as we have seen, wrote that the treaties were not likely to do any great harm since we "would not pay the smallest attention to them in the event of their being invoked in any matter where our interests were seriously involved."[56] Yet he denounced Germany for her violation of a treaty obligation in respect to Belgian neutrality. Bryan thanked God that Roosevelt did not speak for the American people. It is noteworthy that Roosevelt did admit that a violation of the treaties would be morally damaging, and that before his death he was ready to say that, as far as Great Britain went, we could assume that there could arise no disputes which could not be settled peacefully.[57]

Foreign diplomats and statesmen came to think increasingly well of the Bryan treaties. Although Germany and Austria ac-

[51] Lane to Bryan, Oct. 6, 1919, *Bryan Papers*, 34.

[52] *Saturday Evening Post*, Dec. 6, 1913, 70.

[53] Ross A. Collins to President Harding, Aug. 17, 1921, *Bryan Papers*, 23.

[54] Hon. George Gray to E. Frank Carson, Wilmington, Del., Oct. 12, 1914, *Miscellaneous Letters*, 1914-1923, *Bryan Papers*.

[55] *Current History Magazine*, XXII, Sept., 1925, 860.

[56] New York *Times*, Oct. 4, 1914.

[57] George Haven Putnam, *Review of Reviews*, 59, Jan., 1919, 155.

cepted their idea "in principle," they did not negotiate treaties. The Kaiser, according to Colonel House, said that Germany's strength lay in being always prepared for war at a second's notice, and that she would never sign such a treaty, at the same time paying tribute to its effectiveness by admitting that delay would play into the hands of the enemy by lessening Germany's relative advantage.[58]   The German ambassador, Count von Bernstorff, reminded by Bryan every time they met that his government had not fallen in with his treaty plan, came to regret that the foreign office had taken this position. "If the treaty had been signed by us," he later wrote, "it would most probably have facilitated the negotiations about the U-boat campaign."   Dr. Constantin Dumba, the Austrian-Hungarian ambassador, later thought that the *Lusitania* crisis of May, 1915, would never have become so acute, and that possibly our entrance into the war might have been avoided, had Germany ratified such a treaty.[59]   Similarly Colonel House testified that had Germany signed such a treaty, it would not have been possible for the United States to enter the war on the submarine issue until after the lapse of a year, except on the ground that Germany's use of the submarine constituted an act of war against the United States.[60]   The *Tageblatt* held that the declaration of war would probably have been prevented had the German government negotiated a Bryan treaty with America.[61]   Certainly Germany's decision played into the hands of allied propagandists who pointed to her refusal as evidence of a warlike and aggressive character.   Josephus Daniels in 1920 could say that Germany's unwillingness in 1914 to commit herself to the Bryan plan was a forecast of her action in precipitating war.[62]   It was to Bryan's

[58] Charles Seymour, *The Intimate Papers of Colonel House*, (Boston, 1926), I, 256 n.
[59] Count Johann von Bernstorff, *My Three Years in America* (N. Y., 1920), 27; Constantin Dumba, *Memoirs of a Diplomat*, (Boston, 1932), 229. Bryan learned in confidence that Germany would like to have made such a treaty with United States, but feared it might set a precedent which would annoy her in dealing with neighboring nations. Bryan to Wayne Williams, Jan. 26, 1923, *Bryan Papers*, 35.
[60] Seymour, *loc. cit.*
[61] New York *Times*, Apr. 7, 1917.
[62] *Ibid.*, Jan. 9, 1920.

credit that he did not point this out, or resent the action of Powers refusing to accept his treaties.[63]

Although President Poincaré publicly said that Bryan's peace plan appealed to him,[64] the French government only reluctantly instructed Jusserand to negotiate a treaty. Jusserand observed to his British colleague in Washington that, under the proposed treaty, neither France nor England could obtain redress by force, in case of an American occupation of their territory, until after a favorable decision by the commission.[65] Clearly there was no great enthusiasm in his note to Bryan when the treaty with France was finally signed.[66]

Great Britain's attitude was, at first, only slightly more favorable. Our Mexican policy brought us no popularity in London; and, in addition, there were obstacles in the way of a renewal of our old arbitration treaty, which had expired. Above all else, however, our attitude towards the Canal Tolls Exemption Act, by which our shipping in the Panama canal was given preference, aroused great indignation in England, whose government insisted that the Exemption Act violated the Hay-Pauncefote treaty. Bryan had favored the Canal Tolls Exemption Act, and his influence was bound to be important in the question of its repeal, which he at first opposed.[67] Sir Cecil Spring-Rice, the British ambassador in Washington, was not slow to see that Bryan's pet treaty plan might be used as a lever to win his support for the repeal of the Tolls Exemption Act. Speaking of the American secretary of state's "profound and haunting desire" to get his treaties consummated, the British ambassador counselled his government: "If you

[63] Sir Cecil Spring-Rice to Bryan, Dec. 17, 1916, *Bryan Papers*, 36.
[64] *The Commoner*, 14, Aug., 1914, 22.
[65] Stephen Gwynn, *The Letters and Friendships of Sir Cecil Spring-Rice*, II, 206.
[66] Jusserand to Bryan, Oct. 8, 1914, *Bryan Papers*, 36.
[67] David F. Houston, *Eight Years in Wilson's Cabinet*, (N. Y., 1926), II, 59. Bryan at first opposed repeal, partly because the party platform had promised exemption to American shipping, and partly because he suspected the transcontinental railroads were behind the movement for repeal. Many senators opposed the renewal of the arbitration treaty because they did not wish the tolls question to be arbitrated. Ray Stannard Baker, *Woodrow Wilson Life and Letters* (N. Y., 1931), IV, 400.

want to gain him (for a time), help them on, and you will have your reward."[68]   On February 17, Spring-Rice went even further in urging London to exploit the connection between the peace treaties and the canal tolls affair.[69]   Although he had no great faith in the value of the Bryan treaty, he continued to advise his government to begin negotiations.[70]   In London, Page, our ambassador, likewise reminded Grey as frequently as he thought it courteous of Bryan's eagerness to have such a treaty with England.[71]

By the end of March, 1914, Bryan was thought to have changed his position on the Canal Tolls Exemption Act.   On March 28, he was quoted in Congress as favoring repeal;[72] and a fortnight later he was commended in an editorial in the New York *Times* for his position.[73]   Bryan now thought that repeal, which he had consistently opposed, was a necessary recognition of the sanctity of our engagement under the Hay-Pauncefote treaty of 1901.   On March 31 the House repealed the act discriminating in favor of our shipping; and on June 11 the Senate likewise did so.   Bryan's influence in the repeal was not negligible.

Meanwhile Page informed Bryan, about the middle of March, that negotiations for a treaty were at last under way, and that its final consummation might be regarded as certain.   His words were full of meaning:

"This is a great gain—a long journey from the place we stood a few months ago.   Then, I am sure, this Government would hardly have considered this treaty.   They would have used it to bring pressure on us to renew the old arbitration treaty and to repeal the discriminating canal tolls clause.   The arbitration treaty being renewed and the President's eloquent Message having been spoken, they at once took up the Peace Treaty.   It is only fair to Sir Edward Grey to say that he has always been favorable to it, but

[68] *Letters of Sir Cecil Spring-Rice,* II, 201.
[69] *Ibid.,* 202.
[70] *Ibid.,* 206.
[71] Page to Bryan, Mar. 17, 1914, *Correspondence,* 28.
[72] *Cong. Record,* 51, Pt. 6, 63 Cong., 2 sess., 5677, 5708, 5736, 5760.   As late as April 15, however, Bryan seemed disposed, at a meeting of the cabinet, to defend exemption.   Ray Stannard Baker, *op. cit.,* IV, 400.
[73] New York *Times,* Mar. 28, editorial Apr. 14, 1914, recognizing Bryan's contribution to the repeal.

I do not believe he could have got it out of the Cabinet till these other things were cleared up."[74]

Thus the Bryan treaty for the promotion of world peace was used by England as a diplomatic pawn to secure trade advantages. During the early summer of 1914 the negotiations dragged, complicated as they were by the necessity of consulting the Dominions and by the desire on the part of Great Britain to make sure of the direct and immediate reference to the commission of any difficulty that might threaten war, without the interposition of any elective body.[75] Sir Cecil Spring-Rice pointed out to Bryan that unless it could be made certain that the Senate would not interpret the treaty as giving it a right to decide whether or not a given question was to be referred to the commission, the whole scheme would fall to the ground. If the Senate insisted on that right, then Parliament and the legislative bodies of the Dominions would reciprocally demand it; and this would be most unfortunate in view of the fact that the essence of the plan was to withdraw a burning question from contact with combustible material.[76] Bryan agreed with the British ambassador that a treaty of doubtful interpretation on this point might be worse than no treaty at all, and skillfully managed the matter by sending to every senator a statement calling attention to the fact that the treaties contemplated the submission of disputes to investigation without further authority from the Senate. Surprisingly, no objection came from the members of that jealous and sensitive body,[77] and the treaties were finally ready for ratification when the world war broke out. It looked as if the whole matter of ratification would be postponed by the British government, for on September 1, 1914, Page wrote that while Sir Edward Grey had promised to do what he could to

[74] Page to Bryan, Mar. 7, 1914, *Correspondence,* 28.

[75] Sir Cecil Spring-Rice to Bryan, London, June 17, 1914; Spring-Rice to Bryan, July 13, 1914; Spring-Rice to Bryan, July 21, 1914, *Bryan Papers,* 36. Japan, an ally of Britain, smoothed the difficulty in the way of England's acceptance of the Bryan treaty raised by a possible war between United States and Japan. Viscount Grey of Fallodon, *Twenty-Five Years* (N. Y., 1925) II, 104.

[76] Bryan to Sir Cecil Spring-Rice, June 30, 1914, Aug. 24, 1914, *ibid.*

[77] Page to Bryan, London, Sept. 1, 1914, *Bryan Papers,* 34.

further the treaty, it was unlikely that anything would be accomplished until the war was over. Then, suddenly on September 15, the treaty was ratified.[78]

It seems plain that the British ratification of the treaty on September 15, and the similar action of France on the same day, was connected with a desire to impress American opinion with the pacific intention of the Allies, in contrast to Germany's militarism. That there was need of this in the eyes of the British government is clear from the fact that the Allies' agreement of September 5 to fight to the end without making a separate peace, dimmed American hopes for an early end of the war. On the same day Oscar Straus, an eminent American diplomat, rushed to Washington to tell Bryan that the German ambassador, Bernstorff, believed Germany to be ready to negotiate peace.[79] Sir Cecil Spring-Rice and Jusserand were at once informed of Bernstorff's remark, and Jusserand felt convinced that the German ambassador must be speaking on the authority of Berlin. On September 8 Bryan cabled our ambassadors in London, Paris and Berlin of Germany's apparent move for mediation. Our representatives in those capitals replied that the Allies would not hear to negotiations;[80] Gerard, our ambassador to Germany, regarded her somewhat noncommittal reply as leaving open the door to mediation.[81] The American press in part reflected the impression that while Germany was ready to make peace, the Allies were responsible for continuing the war.[82] In London, Page frankly confessed to Sir Edward Grey his fear that the German move, coming on top of the announced Allied agreement to make no separate peace, would convince American opinion that the Allies were responsible for blocking the possibility of an early peace.[83] On September 8, Sir Cecil Spring-Rice urged

[78] *Foreign Relations of the United States,* 1914, 304-307.
[79] Count Bernstorff, *My Three Years in America,* 68-69; *Letters of Sir Cecil Spring-Rice,* II, 221-222; Oscar S. Straus, *Under Four Administrations* (Boston, 1922), 378 ff.
[80] *Foreign Relations, 1914, Supplement,* 100-101.
[81] *Ibid.,* 104.
[82] New York *Times,* Sept. 8, 1914; *Literary Digest,* 49, Sept. 19, 1914, 493-495; Bernstorff, *My Three Years in America,* 69.
[83] Viscount Grey, *Twenty-five Years,* II, 119-120.

Grey to weaken this impression by an Allied declaration for a permanent peace with guarantees.[84] Then, on September 15, England and France signed the Bryan treaties which Page, only a fortnight before, felt convinced would lie unratified until after the conclusion of the war. While there is no direct evidence that this decision was due to a desire to win American opinion, it is entirely likely that such was the case. If this is true, the Bryan treaties with England and France were entered into somewhat ingeniously by those Powers to further their own war ends rather than sincerely to promote the cause Bryan meant to serve.

It is due Sir Cecil Spring-Rice to say, however, that he later regarded with respect the essential principle in the Bryan treaties. On October 6, 1914, he wrote Bryan:

"It may be that some people at first spoke lightly of your idea. No one who has studied the diplomatic history of the events leading to the present disastrous war can ever speak lightly of your idea again. For it is abundantly manifest that even one week's enforced delay would probably have saved the peace of the world."[85]

Moreover, when the diplomatic situation between England and the United States became increasingly delicate, the British ambassador pleaded with his government for a "little forebearance," calling attention to the fact that the Bryan treaty in any case provided "machinery for preventing the dispute from becoming too acrimonious."[86] In April, 1915, Spring-Rice urged Sir Edward Grey to avoid giving offence to the United States, since Americans, in view of the Bryan treaty, regarded a quarrel with England as less serious than one with Germany.[87] It is significant, too, that Wilson's note of May 9, 1916 to Germany was accompanied by a statement from Lansing that we were acting in our dealings with Great Britain "as we are unquestionably bound to act" in view of

[84] *Letters*, II, 223.
[85] Sir Cecil Spring-Rice to Bryan, Washington, Oct. 6, 1914, *Bryan Papers, Correspondence*, 28. Sir Cecil Spring-Rice repeated this sentiment in a letter dated December 17, 1916, *Bryan Papers*, 36.
[86] *Letters of Sir Cecil Spring-Rice*, II, 236.
[87] *Ibid.*, 345.

the explicit treaty engagement with that Government—a treaty we had offered to Germany in vain.[88]   This statement attracted much interest in both England and Germany, the point being emphasized that the United States and England could not, in their differences, come to blows without a breathing spell.[89]

On other occasions, too, when relations with Great Britain were distressing, the Bryan treaty played a part.   In August, 1916, Sir Cecil Spring-Rice warned his government that a breaking point in the relations of the two countries might come at any moment. In case it did, he advised the British to appeal to the Bryan treaty.[90]   Indeed, we almost had to accept England's suggestion to delay action regarding her encroachments on our neutral rights. We were cut off from precipitate action even had we elected to take such a course.   The Bryan treaties were never formally tested in the critical period of our relations with England, but they were not without influence.[91]

If the Bryan treaty was but one factor in preventing a war between England and the United States during the trying year of 1916, the influence of the treaties on the peace machinery erected after the war is clearly established.   The principle of abstention from hostilities during a period of investigation and attempted conciliation, provided for by Article 12 of the Covenant of the

[88] New York *Times*, May 9, 1916.

[89] *Ibid.*, May 15, 1916; Bernstorff, *My Three Years in America*, 264 ff.

[90] Spring-Rice to Grey, Sept. 15, 1916, *op. cit.* II, 348-349.   When Wilson requested the Neutrality Board to advise a course of action which would compel Great Britain to observe its neutral duties towards us, the naval members agreed on a joint report.   Dr. James Brown Scott, however, was unable to assent because he thought their recommendations contrary to the Bryan treaty with Great Britain, and later expressed the opinion that perhaps the Treaty was responsible for the preservation of peace between the two countries.   (Typewritten report of the remarks made by Dr. James Brown Scott at a meeting of the American Society of International Law, April 26, 1929.)   But in so far as it was responsible for Wilson's decision to drop the question of compelling British respect for our neutral rights, it made war with Germany the more likely.

[91] Although no action had ever been taken on any of these treaties for the settlement of a dispute, Calvin Coolidge in 1928 advised the appointment of commissioners for the international permanent commissions set up by the Bryan treaties.   New York *Times*, May 15, 1928.

League of Nations, is plainly the principle of the Bryan treaties.[92]
Indeed, when Dr. James Brown Scott sent a copy of the Bryan
treaties to the Nobel Prize Committee, he accompanied it with the
statement that "the peace treaty plan was made the chief corner
stone of the League of Nations."[93] In September, 1922, the As-
sembly of the League adopted a plan of conciliation which was in
its essentials the plan of the Bryan treaties.[94] During Dr.
Scott's services to the Committee of Jurists which at The Hague formed
a plan for a permanent court of international justice, he presented
to each member of the committee a copy of the volume containing
the Bryan treaties. When the project for a Court was formulated,
the committee unanimously adopted as Article 39 the phraseology
of Article 4 of Bryan's treaties with China, France and Sweden.[95]

In 1923, at the Central American Conference, a convention for
the establishment of international commissions of inquiry was
signed.[96] Professor Shotwell has pointed out that the principle of
reference to a commission of conciliation is carried a step further
in the Locarno treaties,[97] which depart from the Bryan treaties
only in not leaving "liberty of action" to the parties after the
report of the commission. In an important sense, the Bryan principle also became part of the Four Power Treaty negotiated in
1922 between Japan, Great Britain, France and the United
States.[98] In 1928 the idea of the Bryan treaty was again incorporated in a new Franco-American arbitration treaty.[99] By accus-
toming the governments of great nations to the idea of renouncing
war for the period of a year, the Bryan treaties for the advancement of peace prepared the way for the Pact of Paris by which

[92] David Hunter Miller, *The Drafting of the Covenant* (New York and
London, 1928), I, 27, 32, 326. See also Josephus Daniels in the New York
Times, Jan. 9, 1920.
[93] James Brown Scott to Bryan, May 19, 1920, *Bryan Papers*, 22.
[94] John Bassett Moore to Bryan, Geneva, Sept. 29, 1922, *Bryan Papers*, 28.
[95] George N. Finch to Bryan, Washington, Sept. 11, 1920, *Bryan Papers*,
18.
[96] James Brown Scott to Bryan, March 3, 1923, *Bryan Papers*, 19.
[97] James T. Shotwell, *War as an Instrument of National Policy*, (N. Y.,
1929), 122, 265, 259.
[98] Bryan to Wayne Williams, Jan. 26, 1923. *Bryan Papers*, 35.
[99] Shotwell, *op. cit.*, 123.

war was renounced as a national policy, for obviously if war could be renounced for one year, it could be for five years, ten years, or any unlimited period of years.[100] The realization that his work was finding broader expression in the new post-war peace machinery was a comfort to Bryan in his political isolation.[101] He felt with some truth that he had once more given to others an idea which they were permitted to give a wider application. Bryan thus again saw ideas of his own, once ridiculed, now translated by others into realities.

[100] James Brown Scott, Remarks at the meeting of the American Society of International Law, April 26, 1929, typewritten report.
[101] *Memoirs of William Jennings Bryan,* 387, 394.

III

A PACIFIST IN HIGH OFFICE

Apart from negotiating his thirty treaties, Bryan had other opportunities, during his two years and three months as secretary of state, to stand by and promote his peace principles, more than once severely tested by concrete realities. When he finally resigned, Colonel House thought that, more than any other one person, he had endangered the security of his country by a "peace-at-any-price policy."[1] Did his policy deserve this indictment? Did he really put peace before everything else? Was he consistently applying his principles of love and the golden rule in every situation and problem? Did he refrain under all sorts of provocation from threatening force, or sanctioning its use, to effect his ends? And if so, then was Colonel House right in his judgment that Bryan's pacific policy defeated the cause he had at heart?

Bryan's behavior under trial illuminates not only his own character, but also the weakness and strength of his peace principles and technique. To be sure, many serious handicaps not necessarily associated with those principles hindered his efforts to apply effectively his ideas to diplomacy. In the first place, Bryan was by no means his own master: he did not exert as much influence over foreign policy as have a great many secretaries of state. It was said at the time, and has constantly been said since, that Wilson was his own secretary of state. He had expressed the conviction in his *Constitutional Government of the United States* that "the initiative in foreign affairs, which the President possesses without any restriction whatever, is virtually the power to control them absolutely,"[2] and he acted pretty consistently on that principle. In some matters, notably the peace treaties and Caribbean affairs, Wilson gave his secretary of state a fairly free hand: but in general Bryan was a first lieutenant carrying out his captain's policies,

---

[1] Charles Seymour, *The Intimate Papers of Colonel House,* II, 86.
[2] Quoted by Ray Stannard Baker, *Woodrow Wilson, Life and Letters,* IV, 55.

sometimes influencing them, but more often being influenced by them. Only rarely was he unable to agree with his chief. Hardly more than a month after the inauguration the newspapers were full of stories to the effect that the President was ignoring Bryan and his office. He therefore took the Washington correspondent of the Philadelphia *Public Ledger* into his confidence and reassured the country in regard to the sympathetic unity of the President and himself on all matters of importance in foreign policy. (This, indeed, was true.) He had found the President "altogether fair," and had never known a man with "a more open mind nor one who tried more sincerely to get at the meat of any question."[3]   Yet Wilson constantly wrote important instructions which ordinarily the Secretary of State would draft; kept in close touch with foreign governments, and with our ambassadors abroad, through Colonel House, with the result that Bryan often did not know what was going on, or what the President's position really was; and the President, on at least one occasion, announced a consequential decision in the cabinet which involved the Secretary of State, without even having consulted him beforehand.[4]   In spite of this, as well as many efforts to make trouble between them, Wilson had both confidence in and an affectionate admiration for Bryan, whose sincerity, transparent integrity, Christian principle, tact in dealing with men of many sorts, capacity for business, and mastery of the principles of each matter he dealt with, cleared away many difficulties and gave to "the policy of the State Department a definiteness and dignity that are very admirable."[5]   It was this attitude which made Bryan's position tolerable by giving him some opportunity to influence the administration. We may therefore judge his consistency to his peace principles in situations in which he had reasonable freedom. Yet it is important not to forget that in major policies Bryan had to follow rather than lead. Many who have criticized his inconsistencies have forgotten that.

[3] Philadelphia *Public Ledger,* cited in Springfield *Republican,* Apr. 23, 1913.
    [4] Bryan to Daniels, Mar. 11, 1924, *Bryan Papers,* 35.
    [5] Wilson to W. L. Marbury, quoted in Ray Stannard Baker, *Woodrow Wilson, Life and Letters,* IV, 406-407.

In addition to the fact that Bryan's freedom was thus greatly restricted, still other considerations, not necessarily inherent in his peace principles, handicapped his efforts to apply them effectively to diplomacy. Schooled in politics and chautauqua, he was unused to the ways of diplomacy. Walter Hines Page, irritated by his informal way of dashing off notes of introduction for Tom, Dick and Harry to the highest English officials, bitterly complained of his carelessness in not promptly answering really important letters.[6] The irritation Page felt made him all the less ready to coöperate with Bryan in his efforts to convince London that we were really in earnest in our protests against British violations of our neutral rights. Bryan's mind, moreover, was political and moral rather than legal. Few public men had made more enemies than he during his long career, and no one in the administration owed as many debts to "deserving Democrats" as he did with his six million supporters who had stood by him through thick and thin. It would be useless to deny that some of his appointments were unfortunate and hindered the peaceful purposes he cherished. It would be equally useless to deny that diplomats and foreign officials thought of him with scant respect, though some who came to know him well did cherish affection, and even respect, for him. House and Page, however, again and again reported the smiles and condescensions his name provoked whenever it was mentioned in official circles in Europe's capitals.[7] What derision and abuse his chautauqua lectures during his vacations brought![8] What laughs

[6] Mr. Baker points out that Bryan might well have argued that Page was being directly informed by the President and Colonel House, and that it was hence not necessary to answer his letters, *Woodrow Wilson, Life and Letters,* IV, 297.

[7] Seymour, *op. cit.,* I, 269, 274, 282, 236.

[8] Bryan did not disclose the fact that the President approved of his utilizing his vacations for chautauqua lectures if he chose. In Europe, Bryan found a valiant defender in the Baronness von Suttner, who wrote in the *Neue Freie Presse* of the effective work done in the chautauqua and called attention to the fact that eminent Americans, such as ex-President Taft and P. P. Claxton, U. S. Commissioner of Education, had appeared before chautauquas which were far from being the variety shows visioned by Europe. *Advocate of Peace,* lxxv, Nov., 1913, 227-229. Bryan's chautauqua work in part, at least, was education for peace.

occasioned by the serving of grape juice at diplomatic dinners—
the shackling of Bacchus; what ridicule his peace projects and
pacific diplomacy aroused among army and navy men, and in the
press—the shackling of Mars![9]   In addition to all this, Bryan's
relations with newspaper men were not happy: they expected this
democrat of democrats to share official secrets generously, and
begrudged the fact that he was a stickler for secrecy.[10] Yet in
spite of this there were constant "leaks" in his department which
brought him severe criticism.

Before considering Bryan's specific actions, it is worth noting
that his influence was often used against militarism in councils of
state.   On one occasion, when Garrison, secretary of war, observed
that the views of the cabinet on army and navy matters were of no
importance, the Secretary of State flared up. Very emphatically,
with flushed face, he thundered out that the views of army and
navy officers could not be trusted as to what should be done or not
done until we were actually at war. The point was, Bryan insisted,
not how to wage war, but how to avoid war. If ships were moved
about in the Orient, as some desired, conflict with Japan, which
was a serious possibility, would be invited. Wilson, knowing that
he would be bitterly criticized if war should come and preparations
had not been made, was in this instance guided by Bryan in announcing that he would direct the ships to remain in their present
position.[11]

At the farewell dinner to Ambassador Bryce on April 24, 1913,
Bryan came out strongly for progressive disarmament and appealed particularly to England, France, Germany and his own
country to take the initiative.[12]   In the autumn of 1914 he had an
opportunity for showing his colors as far as his own government
went.   House called his opposition to plans for increasing the
military strength of the country through the reserve plan violent

[9] Arthur Wallace Dunn, *From Harrison to Harding.* II, 230; New York
Times, Apr. 23, 1913.
[10] Dunn, *op. cit.,* 227-228, 230.
[11] Houston, *Eight Years in Wilson's Cabinet.* I, 66-67.
[12] *La paix par le Droit,* 23 anneé, 10 mai, 1913, no. 9, 293-294; New York
Times, Apr. 25, 1913.

and naïve, and feared he might make trouble.[13] On another occasion Bryan blocked the plans of the navy department to equip a hospital ship for which there were ample funds, lest our act be interpreted as a warlike preparation.[14] Yet the Secretary of State was no mere theorist. He was willing not to push his convictions if there was no reasonable opportunity for their realization. He did not think it practical, for example, to support a resolution introduced by a Missouri Democrat in the House calling on the administration to inaugurate measures for a coöperative naval holiday among the leading maritime Powers. "It would be difficult," he wrote to the President, "to agree on a year for a naval holiday because of the contracts different nations have already made. The idea is good, but it would not seem to me practicable."[15]

Realizing the importance of international coöperation as a means to peace, Bryan did all he could to further it. Early in his secretaryship he prepared a report urging an appropriation from Congress for an American delegation to the Second Opium Conference. National action alone could not eradicate such an evil, Bryan insisted, and therefore "the coöperation of all the states directly and indirectly interested" was indispensable if progress were to be made in questions which, like this one, were international in their moral, humanitarian, economic and diplomatic aspects.[16] It was, of course, The Hague Conferences which promised most for international coöperation, and convinced of the importance of an early meeting at The Hague, the Secretary of State did all he could to make one possible. When the advisory committee, appointed on June 10, 1912, made its preliminary report on agenda, Bryan sought Wilson's approval for asking the Queen of the Netherlands to invite the nations to The Hague in 1915.[17] On

[13] Seymour, op. cit., I, 300.
[14] New York Times, Jan. 11, 1915.
[15] Cong. Record, 51, Pt. 6, 1 sess., 5830 ff., Oct. 18, 1913; Bryan to Wilson, Mar. 13, 1914, Bryan Letter Books.
[16] Foreign Relations of the United States, 1913, 218.
[17] Bryan to Wilson, Jan. 28, 1914, Bryan Letter Books. Bryan thought that the Conference should be held in 1915 rather than in 1916 partly because of the greater freedom in the selection of delegates in a non-campaign year.

January 1, 1914, our diplomatic agents were instructed to facilitate the preparation of the next conference.[18]   Meantime Bryan was very anxious to prevent the military and naval elements from dominating the committee appointed at home to prepare further plans for the conference. "However interested they may be in the peace movement," he reminded the President, "their connection with the War Department and the Navy Department would make it very difficult for them to consider the proposition from the same standpoint as the civilian."[19]   In view of the failure of the Tripartite Naval Conference at Geneva in 1927, the wisdom of his position is plain. But, inasmuch as several important Powers insisted that they could not carry through the necessary inquiries and studies relative to agenda as early as 1915, Bryan reluctantly had to abandon his hope that the conference assemble that year. He did, however, fix June, 1916, as the definite date for its meeting. The outbreak of war in August, 1914 once more defeated his plans.[20]

Disappointed in his purpose of inaugurating the third Hague Conference, Bryan also failed to realize another plan for peace by virtue of events over which he had no control. He had hoped that the centennial year of Anglo-American peace might be celebrated in such a way as to deepen friendly relations between the two countries, and at the same time present to other nations a powerful example of two peoples solving serious differences during a century by peaceful means. But Page in London resented his way of handling the proposed demonstration; the House of Representatives defeated the appropriation for the celebration of the century of peace;[21] and England presently had on her hands a war on the continent.

[18] *Foreign Relations of the United States, 1914,* 4-5. A national citizens' committee, composed of distinguished Americans, was formed in Feb., 1914, to further an early meeting of the Conference. New York *Times,* Feb. 13, 1914.

[19] Bryan to Wilson, Mar. 10, 1914, *Bryan Letter Books.*

[20] *Foreign Relations,* 1914, 10-11.

[21] Bryan to Whitelaw Reid, June 30, 1914, *Bryan Papers,* 36; John Stewart, chairman of the Sulgrave Institution, to Bryan, Aug. 25, 1921, *Bryan Papers,* 22; Hendricks, *Letters of Walter Hines Page,* (Garden City, 1922-1925), I, 235-6.

While these defeats must have been painful, Bryan compensated as best he could by receiving pacifist delegations, foreign and American, at the State Department;[22] addressing organizations on the question of peace; and pushing his treaty plan. It was something to have a secretary of state who used his office to educate the public in peace. "Our most pronounced pacifists," observed the *Advocate of Peace,* "have never expressed themselves more definitely than has our Secretary of State."[23]

But Bryan did not always act as he spoke. He took but little interest in the administration's Pan-American policy, which visioned a permanent association of American nations. The President blamed him for not pushing the Pan-American Pact which, with Colonel House, he was fondly nourishing; Colonel House himself could not understand his propensity for lagging in the matter.[24] The truth is that it came to be a pet project of the Colonel's, and Bryan was quite willing to let him play with his own toy. As for himself, he had his treaties which he regarded as both important and adequate. To be sure, he hoped that the House project might be used to promote greater coöperation among the American Powers in defining and defending neutral rights in war time, and in itself this proved that he was not indifferent to Pan-Americanism. As a matter of fact, he had often advocated it, and continued to do so.[25]

Still, it remained true that he often failed to act as if he understood economic imperialism, which had led to the use on our part of military force and which had been widening the misunderstanding between the Americas. At times he actually lent his hand to

[22] John Mez, Dec. 29, 1921, to Bryan, *Misc. Letters,* 1914-1923; Sir Cecil Spring-Rice to Bryan. June 23. 1913, *Bryan Papers,* 36.

[23] *Advocate of Peace,* LXXVI, June, 1914, 128-129; LXXV, July, 1913, 146-147.

[24] Seymour, *op. cit.,* I, 207 ff., II, 18-19. As a matter of fact, it was Bryan who seems first to have suggested to Wilson the idea of a non-aggression Pan-American Pact. Baker, *op. cit.,* IV, 285.

[25] *American Secretaries of State,* X, 20-21. Bryan urged Carnegie to endow chairs of American history and government in South American universities for the promotion of better relations between the two Americas. Bryan to Carnegie, Jan. 7, 1915, *Correspondence,* 1913-1925.

further its development. The great anti-imperialist of 1900 had clearly seen many of the economic implications of colonialism; now, when cloaked somewhat differently, he often failed to recognize them. In view of some of his acts which were inconsistent with his peace principles, it is worth inquiring to what extent the Great Commoner really understood the technique and implications of economic imperialism.

Three days after the inauguration, the cabinet listened to the President discuss the general Latin American situation. The discussion was based on a typewritten statement which Wilson had himself prepared, and which declared that the United States had nothing to seek in Central and South America except "the lasting interests of the peoples of the two continents, the security of governments intended for the people and for no special group or interest, and the development of personal and trade relationships between the two continents which shall redound to the profit and advantage of both and interfere with the rights and liberties of neither."[26] This was a frank repudiation of "dollar diplomacy" and Bryan listened with a smile on his face and nodded approval as the President read.[27] On March 12 Wilson's statement appeared in the press. In an interview with a correspondent of the New York *World* on April 20, 1913, Bryan elaborated and approved the policy of the President regarding the repudiation of dollar diplomacy.[28]

Bryan could act as well as talk. At his initiative a representative of an American corporation in Ecuador whose conduct as an arbitrator in a controversy between the American concessionaires and the government of that country had displeased the latter, was replaced by a more impartial person.[29] Honduras was also gratified by the administration's refusal to support a certain loan which would have bound her body and soul.[30] Moreover, Bryan brought to the President's attention, only a few days before his Mobile

[26] Baker, *Woodrow Wilson*, IV, 66-67.
[27] Houston, *op. cit.*, I, 43-44.
[28] Baker, *op. cit.*, IV.
[29] *Memoirs*, 365-366.
[30] *Ibid.*, 364.

address, one of the points he especially emphasized: the exploitation of our southern neighbors by our bankers.[31]   Indeed, it did not take the Secretary of State long to see through the bankers' practice of lending money for large securities and high interest rates, then demanding that their government eliminate the risk for which they had charged by backing them in emergencies.   Was there no way out, short of a repudiation of capitalism itself? Bryan saw that on the one hand the Latin American states needed our money for railroads and education, and that, failing to get it from us, they would turn to Europe.   That might involve us in intervention to defend the Monroe Doctrine.   On the other hand, it seemed hardly fair for our bankers to charge exorbitant rates and at the same time fasten their control on weaker states, goading them to revolution in order to free themselves, or else condemning them to chafe under actual American intervention for the protection of our interests.

By the middle of the summer of 1913 Bryan had thought of a way out.   It was for our government to extend its credit to Latin American states:

". . . If the United States offers to loan them its credit to the extent that such a loan is safe, the bonds could be made to draw four and a half per cent., which would be an immediate saving to them in the way of interest and the difference of a (per) cent. and a half between their bonds and ours could go into a sinking fund which would, in a reasonable time, at compound interest, pay off the debt and leave them free.   We could, in this way, relieve them of the debts which embarrass them, and enable them to construct such railroads as are imperatively necessary for the development of their countries.   The second advantage would be that the plan would give our country such an increased influence . . . that we could prevent revolutions, promote education, and advance stable and just government . . . we would in the end profit, negatively, by not having to incur expense in guarding our own and foreign interests there, and, positively, by the increase of trade that would come from development and from the friendship which would follow the conferring of the benefits named."[32]

[31] Ibid.
[32] Baker, op. cit., IV, 433-434, quoting a letter from Bryan to Wilson, Aug. 6, 1913.

But Wilson would have none of this "novel and radical" plan. He thought the bankers would grant easier terms than they had insisted on in the unratified Knox-Castrillo treaty.

Unable to persuade the bankers to relent and offer the harassed government of Nicaragua easier terms, Bryan hit on what he hoped would prove to be a solution. If we could obtain by treaty an option on the canal site and a virtual financial protectorate, the bankers' risk would then become so much less great that they would grant easier terms. Such a treaty was actually negotiated while our marines kept in power the Nicaraguan dictator who had favored all along American interests, and who now complacently granted all that was asked. But the treaty, when laid before the Senate committee on foreign relations, ran up against the first of many snags. The minority of the committee opposed the clause providing for a "protectorate" over Nicaragua: it was clear that the Senate would not permit any further extension of authority over that republic. Indeed, it seemed to conservative Republicans that Bryan's treaty made the dollar diplomacy of Knox and Taft look like a milk-and-water affair by contrast. The treaty also aroused the hostility of Costa Rica and Salvador, both of whom felt that it violated the sovereignty of Nicaragua and her treaty obligations with them as well. Even the Central American Court took a similar view. Thus Bryan, who understood the evils of dollar diplomacy and tried to find some other way out, merely avoided one reef and struck another. Moreover, he widened still further the gulf between our Latin American neighbors and ourselves. The remedy had proved worse than the cure; and the situation in Nicaragua remained at least as bad as, and probably worse than, it had been before.[33]

In the republic of Santo Domingo, Bryan's inept minister, James Mark Sullivan, pursued policies leading to misrule and bloodshed.[34] Bryan had given instructions to support the lawful authorities and to discourage any insurrectionary attempts.

[33] *Ibid.*, IV, 436 ff.
[34] *Foreign Relations.* 1914, 193 ff.; Melvin M. Knight, *The Americans in Santo Domingo,* (N. Y., 1928), chap. vi.

Further, insurrectionists were not to be recognized if they succeeded in gaining control : we were to freeze them out by refusing
to pay over to their government the Santo Domingan share of the
customs receipts which we administered. This led to constant
intermeddling in the island's affairs. Against the protests of the
Santo Domingans, their elections were supervised; troublesome
candidates were removed ; in short, all sorts of acts were done for
which we had no legal authority. Bryan and his minister, Sullivan,
truly made confusion worse confounded and Wilson finally had to
take the situation into his own hands.[35] American prestige was
undermined, and the way paved for the later military intervention
and occupation.

When an outbreak occurred in the capital of Haiti, the neighboring republic, Bryan took the conventional course : he asked the
navy department for a warship to proceed immediately to Port-au-
Prince to protect American interests which seemed to be threatened.[36] In October, 1914, Bryan wrote to the President :

"It seemed to me of the first importance that the naval force in
Haitian waters should be at once increased, not only for the purpose of protecting foreign interests but also as evidence of the
intention of this Government to settle the unsatisfactory state of
affairs which exists."[37]

The disciple of Tolstoy, confronted by a concrete problem, did not
hesitate to rely on force to effect an end which he had so often
said could best be achieved by love, charity, and the example of
good-will. When in December, 1914 rumors reached him that
Haitian officials were threatening to remove government funds
from their national bank, an institution actually controlled by a
New York financial group, Bryan sent for representatives of the
latter to discuss the situation in the island republic. It was arranged that at least half a million dollars, the property of the

[35] Sumner Welles, *Naboth's Vineyard,* (N. Y., 1928), II, 717, 735, 736,
926-927.
[36] A. W. Dunn, *op. cit.,* II, 234-235; Franklin D. Roosevelt to the author,
Aug. 22, 1929.
[37] Foreign Policy Association, "The Seizure of Haiti by the United
States", (N. Y., 1922), 4.

Haitian government, should be brought from the Haitian bank to New York, and that a gunboat be requested from the war department for that purpose. Bryan would not listen to the protest of the Haitian minister, but insisted that the seizure of the money by American marines and the use of a gunboat for transferring it to a place of safety was justified by reason of the grave menace to American interests in Haiti. It seems as if this questionable affair was designed to enforce on Haiti an American customs control. While the Secretary of State realized that we were under obligations to protect that country from injustice at the hands of our citizens, he also informed our minister that our obligation to the American people required us to give "all legitimate assistance to American investors" in Haiti.[38]   Years later he declared: "What we did was for the benefit of the people and was not dictated by any pecuniary advantage to us or to any of our citizens."[39]   Perhaps he had forgotten his earlier acts and words; perhaps this was a rationalization.   In any case, the great exponent of moral suasion sanctioned the use of force in financial relations with a sovereign state: the result lent prestige to the war method and greatly deepened Latin American hostility towards us.

On top of all this, Bryan refused to meet the request of the Colombian government to arbitrate differences with her arising from the grievances she felt because of our part in the Panama revolution. After much haggling, the compromise treaty of April 6, 1914, which would have disposed of the controversy over Panama, remained unratified during his term of office.[40]   It should be said that the Senate's failure to ratify the treaty was not to be laid at Bryan's door.

Bryan, at the very beginning of his secretaryship, eagerly shared Wilson's broad condemnation of dollar diplomacy and

[38] *Foreign Relations*, 1914, 390, 372, 356-364. Select Committee on Haiti and Santo Domingo, U. S. Senate, 67 Cong., 1 and 2 sess., 122-123. See also, "William Jennings Bryan" in *American Secretaries of State*, X, 12-13.

[39] Bryan to Benjamin Williams, May 4, 1925, *Bryan Papers*, 35.

[40] *Foreign Relations*, 1913, 286, 308-309, 315, 316. Bryan's unwillingness to meet Colombia's request for arbitration was due to his belief that direct negotiations were preferable to arbitration. His reason is not clear. *Foreign Relations, 1914*, 143. See also *American Secretaries of State*, X, 12.

economic imperialism. He learned a good deal about its workings during his first year in office, particularly because of the free hand he enjoyed in dealing with the Central American and Caribbean republics.[41] His attention was not as yet distracted by the European war. Yet he did not in his acts substantially check the economic imperialism which he was condemning: in some instances, he even furthered it. His use of force in Haiti brought him into the same category with the most pronounced imperialists. He was, in short, not always consistent with his ideals of pacifism and anti-imperialism. Perhaps this was in part due to the fact that under officials in the state department frequently handled matters in such a way as to bring a crisis which then necessitated a show of force or else a complete and difficult back-down. Even so, Bryan was officially responsible for all that went on in his department, and it is difficult on this score to exonerate him. However, the more we learn from psychologists about personality, the less we expect to find consistent adherence to any particular quality or trait. Bryan was no exception. It is, of course, also very doubtful whether economic imperialism, which was so deeply rooted in our system of industrial and financial capitalism, could be at all effectively checked as long as the system itself was maintained. At most, its technique might be refined, its ruthlessness mitigated. Bryan tried to do that and failed.

When it came to the more complex problem of Mexico, Bryan had less opportunity to adhere to or betray his principles, for the President kept a fairly tight grip on the reins. For the most part, Bryan agreed with his chief in what was done.[42] He beheld the mote in his brother's eye, insisting that England's policy in Mexico was solely dictated by a desire to further her own control over Mexican oil. But that did not keep him from seeing the beam in his own eye, as his memorandum on our Mexican policy, submitted

---

[41] Baker, op. cit., IV, passim.

[42] Ibid., IV, 344. Bryan was present, for example, at a conference with the President and Garrison on June 14, 1913, at which the first outright declaration of the administration's Mexican policy was formulated. Baker, op. cit., IV, 254. John Lind, the most important of the President's personal agents in Mexico, was one of Bryan's friends.

to the President on July 19, 1913, indicates. Admitting that
American lives and property were endangered by the tumultuous
civil war in that country, he condemned the use of force for their
protection. That would be putting ourselves on a level with those
nations which have allowed their citizens to go abroad in search
of gain and then sent armies to guarantee the profits sought. "To
do this in the case of Mexico would be to become responsible for
bloodshed in the undertaking and to fasten upon our country the
burden of administering for a generation to come a foreign government over a hostile people to their own injury and to our own
demoralization."[43] Were we to permit Americans in Mexico to
declare war on that people when the constitution clearly reserved
to Congress that right? Bryan proposed the alternative course-
mediation. Confident of its success, he pointed out that it would
insure protection to our property. "In addition to these tangible
and material dangers involved in war, there is the immeasurable
loss of prestige which must come if we can no longer be looked to
as the leader in the peace movement and as the exponent of human
rights, not to speak of our moral responsibility for the lives lost in
such a war." We were, in short, our brother's keeper : but our
acts were to prevent, rather than to provoke and continue bloodshed. And, above all, property interests were not to be put above
human interests. Clearly this was Bryan the pacifist speaking, and
just as clearly he understood the relation between economic imperialism and war.

Bryan was much gratified when on August 27 Wilson appeared
before Congress and laid down the principles and details of his
Mexican policy. It was apparent that his influence on the President's address had been important. Good offices were tendered.
In proposing that Americans in Mexico leave at once with government assistance, Wilson was following Bryan's suggestion that
Americans venturing into business outside the country must take
their own chances. In addition, the President announced that an
embargo on arms from the United States would prevent all parties

[43] Memorandum submitted to the President, July 19, 1913, *Bryan Papers,*
36.

from securing American aid in their fighting. Above all, the President took the line that only patience was needed, and that drastic action could merely complicate matters.[44] "You have raised our international relations upon the highest possible plane—your appeal cannot fail to bring a response from the conscience of the world"[45]—so he wrote the President. And pacifist opinion agreed. The *Advocate of Peace,* organ of the American Peace Society, commented on the message: "Patient, judicial, and serious, the whole delicate situation is handled firmly but with no spirit of the clenched fist." In neighborly friendliness and in sincerity the American government was merely tendering its good offices, leaving the development of events in the hands of those who were attempting to form a rational public opinion in Mexico.[46]

People influential in the peace movement also assured Bryan that watchful waiting was wise and just. One leader with great interests in Mexico wrote that non-intervention was "the only right policy" even for holders of property in that country.[47] George Fred Williams, minister to Greece, who also had property interests in Mexico, likewise highly approved the Wilson-Bryan policy. The refusal to intervene seemed to this diplomat a revolutionary blow at the prevalent diplomacy of exploitation, intrigue and violence; it was, he continued, a new gospel for the nations, one bound to give hope to humanity, certain to mark a new step in the history of civilization. "God bless you both that you refuse to make widows and orphans and suffering and bloodshed and death at the demand of the property interests." Let our country be the leader in exposing the universal sham by which property keeps humanity enslaved; let it be marked, continued this interesting observer, that this Mexican policy was but the natural

[44] Baker, *op. cit.,* IV, 274-5.
[45] Bryan to Wilson, Aug. 27, 1913. *Bryan Papers, 36.*
[46] *Advocate of Peace,* LXXV, Oct., 1913, 207-208. In December, 1913, the *Advocate* was less certain. Pointing out that our acts had amounted to intervention, it frankly raised the question whether and to what extent it was our duty to oust Huerta, even though he clearly opposed the overthrow of peonage and feudal tyranny, the prerequisite to internal peace. LXXV, Dec., 1913, 246 ff.
[47] George Foster Peabody to Bryan, Nov. 28, 1913. *Bryan Papers, 34.*

expansion of the internal policies for which Bryan had struggled during seventeen years.[48]

Bryan, having set a high standard, sometimes lived up to it. He strenuously objected when the Secretary of War, during a cabinet discussion, desired a certain action, pointing out that it would mean war. Garrison, the Secretary, shrugged his shoulders, and Wilson skilfully turned the conversation.[49] On a later occasion, Bryan stood out against Wilson when he proposed to warn Carranza that our support would be withdrawn if he did not compromise with his enemies. The Secretary of State pointed out that such a warning would play into the hands of the reactionary forces and possibly lead to our own intervention. But he did not insist on his position, and, at the very end of his secretaryship, carried out Wilson's desire.[50]

On other and more important occasions he also failed to maintain the high position he and his chief had taken. It was with his consent that the stubborn Huerta was at last virtually threatened with force unless he quickly stood aside and eliminated himself completely from the tangled situation.[51] This threat proving futile, on February 3, 1914, the embargo on arms and munitions was withdrawn in order that Huerta's enemies might be better enabled to put him down. Bryan, it is true, objected to this in a very pointed memorandum, in which he clearly demonstrated that by sending arms into Mexico we invited further bloodshed, in-

[48] George Fred Williams, Athens, Apr. 1, 1914, to Bryan. This is one of the most remarkable letters in the Bryan papers. Its author, a Boston lawyer, member of the 52d Congress, minister to Greece, showed a very realistic insight into the European situation, prophesying the imminency of a general war stimulated by nationalistic and imperialistic ambitions, with particular reference to the Near East; prophesying also that the question of war or peace would be the chief issue in the presidential campaign of 1916. The letter was characterized by a remarkable idealism. Williams also analysed very skillfully the existing situation in Mexico, and offered an interpretation of American history in the post-civil war period quite in the spirit of such historians as Charles A. Beard.

[49] David Lawrence, *The True Story of Woodrow Wilson*, (N. Y., 1924), 150-151.

[50] David Houston, *Eight Years in Wilson's Cabinet*, I, 133-135; *Foreign Relations*, 1915, 694-695.

[51] A. W. Dunn, *From Harrison to Harding*, II, 249-250; *Foreign Relations, 1913*, 856; *Foreign Relations, 1914*, 443-444.

creased the risk to Americans residing there, and thus paved the way for our own intervention.[52] But he did not insist, and our munitions went to Mexico.

Meantime John Lind was urging Bryan and the President to take immediate and positive action in Mexico: either to support Carranza in his rebellion against Huerta, or to intervene and occupy Mexico with our military. O'Shaughnessy, chargé d'affaires, was giving similar advice. On January 15, 1914, Representative Gillett of Massachusetts denounced in the House the Mexican policy of the administration, and laid the responsibility on Secretary Bryan.[53] Senator Fall and others were talking in like vein. Criticism was increasing; trouble seemed imminent in Mexico City.

Then, in April, a somewhat trivial incident took place in Tampico. American naval officers and their crew were arrested at a point where landing had been prohibited, and although they had been released with apologies, Admiral Mayo demanded further amends including a salute of twenty-one guns to our flag. Huerta refused to go the whole way. The President was at White Sulphur Springs, and Bryan on April 10 advised Wilson that Admiral Mayo had taken the only possible course.[54] Additional vessels and marines were thereupon sent to Tampico, and Wilson laid the whole matter before Congress, characterizing it as an affront to the nation. Bryan, instead of trying to restrain his chief, agreed completely with him even though insistence on the course taken by Admiral Mayo threatened war.[55] Huerta's suggestion that the matter be submitted to The Hague for arbitration was rejected by the Secretary of State who had talked so much of the peaceful settlement of disputes.[56]

Great as the tension was, Bryan actually increased it when, late in the night of April 21, 1914, he learned that word had come from Admiral Fletcher asking whether he should use force to prevent the landing at Vera Cruz of a German vessel bearing arms

[52] *Memorandum, Bryan Papers,* 36.
[53] Baker, *op. cit.,* IV, 298-299, 303.
[54] *Foreign Relations of the United States,* 1914, 449.
[55] Bryan to George Derby, Oct. 3, 1921, *Bryan Papers,* 35.
[56] *Foreign Relations,* 1914, 466.

for Huerta. The Secretary of State wakened Wilson and proposed to give the admiral authority to prevent the landing. Even
when the President pointed out that it might lead to war, Bryan
remained firm.[57] Admiral Fletcher was instructed to seize the
customs house and prevent the German vessel from landing.
Irregular fighting resulted, and the city of Vera Cruz was occupied
under the fire of American guns. Mexican indignation against the
United States reached a high point, and Bryan, despite the fact he
looked "white and worn" and appeared to be suffering under a
great strain,[58] seemed to have forgotten his peace principles.

Other pacifists, however, reminded him of their common principles.[59] A wise counsellor pointed out that the Mexican affront
had come, not from the people, but from a usurper, and that we
had already done all we could to vindicate our national honor.[60]
It was somewhat ironical for Andrew Carnegie, who had not
shown himself too tender of human life during his Pittsburgh
and Homestead career, to plead with Bryan during this crisis to
stand by his philosophy of love and peace. The presence of our
troops, Carnegie argued, could only embitter the contest and delay
its settlement. "No foreign nation has any rite to interfere &
decide" the policy of Mexico. "If rival Mexican forces continue
to war upon each other, the President can decide to withdraw &
allow them to fite it out. He is not called upon to sacrifice our
soldiers, not a man of them, no not one."[61] These pleas from the
Pittsburgh iron-master were in marked contrast to a letter from
Cardinal Gibbons, who approved the use of the army and navy if
necessary to restore order in Mexico.[62]

[57] Joseph P. Tumulty, *Woodrow Wilson as I Know Him*, (N. Y., 1921),
151-152; *Foreign Relations*, 1914, 477.
[58] New York *Times*, Apr. 21, 1914, describing the appearance of the
President and Bryan before Congress.
[59] *Advocate of Peace*, LXXXI, describes the resolutions, petitions and
telegrams from peace societies, women's clubs and mass meetings urging
restraint and the preservation of peace. See also *Concord*, May, 1914, 29-30.
[60] George Gray, Wilmington, Apr. 24, 1914, to Bryan, *Bryan Papers*, 34.
[61] Carnegie to Bryan, May 17, 1914, *Bryan Papers*, 34, and June 8, 1914,
Bryan Papers, 36.
[62] James Cardinal Gibbons, Apr. 27, 1914, to Bryan, *Bryan Papers*, 36.
Bryan has been criticized for not making use of the commission of inquiry outlined in his peace plan, but his critics apparently have forgotten

Had Bryan negotiated one of his peace treaties with Mexico, the commission of inquiry might well have been called on to investigate the facts in these disputes and a cooling-off period invoked. Since no such treaty existed, was it asking too much of Bryan to advise, or even insist, that we act in the spirit of his peace plan? Yet he preferred to rely, at least temporarily, on a display of force, and to support the haughty demand of a naval officer which he must have known endangered peace. Pleased though Bryan must have been when a way out of the difficulties was found through the good offices of Argentina, Brazil and Chile, he could not claim with any justification that he had acted consistently with his pacifist principles. While conciliation was accepted rather than war, it was not until force had been tried first.

If Bryan had not been a consistent pacifist in this test, he had been a good party man and a loyal supporter of the President. The line between violence and non-violence was for him a thin and shifting one; and if national honor were affected, he did not hesitate to move the line to permit the use of force. If he must choose between nationalism and pacifism, the choice was clear, however painful it may have been. To be sure he identified the national policy decided upon with justice, and in the long run, with peace itself. The end, peace, he did not betray; he merely altered the means of achieving it. Hence, after his resignation, he again supported the administration when, in the spring of 1916, troops were sent across the Mexican border: the outrage had been a distressing one, and deserved the severest punishment.[63] Not wishing to embarrass the President, he also refused an invitation to an informal peace conference at El Paso called to prevent an outbreak of hostilities.[64] Bryan loved peace indeed, but he had other loyalties as well.

that such a treaty with Mexico had not been negotiated. Jerome Davis, *Contemporary Social Movements.*. (N. Y., 1930), 820.

The Treaty of Guadalupe Hidalgo, which was in force, committed the United States to consider favorably the arbitration of disputes. See M. E. Curti, "Pacifist Propaganda and the Treaty of Guadalupe Hidalgo," *Amer. Hist. Rev.* XXXIII, Apr. 1928, 596 ff.

[63] New York *Times,* Mar. 11, 1916.
[64] *Ibid.,* June 24, 1916.

If the administration failed to repudiate dollar diplomacy in every dealing with our southern neighbors, it made a better record in the case of China. It was chiefly due to Bryan that the government refused to sanction the participation of a group of American bankers in a six-Power loan to China which might have led to forcible intervention in the financial and political affairs of that country. When the representatives of J. Pierpont Morgan and Company came to the state department in March, 1913, and indicated that the bankers were unwilling to enter the consortium without backing from the administration, Bryan might well have followed the advice of the officials in the department who strongly upheld the old policy of governmental support. But he saw dangers in the proposed course of action and refused to give the bankers an official blessing. Inquiries brought out the fact that the conditions of the loan endangered the independence of China, and therefore violated democratic principles in international relations. Bryan also saw that our government might be called on to use force to protect loans.[65] When he reported the conference at a cabinet meeting on March 14, Houston thought "he had no very clear notion of the proposal."[66] This opinion, contradicting as it does Bryan's clear-cut statement of the objections he raised in his conference with the bankers, ought not to be taken without reservation, especially because it lacks supporting evidence from other cabinet members. Possibly Houston was one of the more cautious and conservative cabinet members who questioned the wisdom of the new policy, and therefore felt Bryan to be somewhat muddle-headed in his position. At the next cabinet meeting Bryan presented a report, and Wilson a statement, which were accepted after a discussion. As a result, American bankers did not participate in the loan. This virtual withdrawal of support given by the Taft administration was for a time fatal to this particular American enterprise in China[67] and won the enthusiastic approval of that country. True, this decision on the part of the administra-

---

[65] *Memoirs of William Jennings Bryan*, 362-363.
[66] Houston, *Eight Years in Wilson's Cabinet*, I, 43.
[67] Herbert Croly, *Willard Straight* (N. Y., 1925), 452-453.

tion did not keep Wilson from sanctioning Japanese aggressions in China in 1917. Nor did it demonstrate that moral force was capable of preventing economic penetration and control of a country:[68] five years later a state department which took orders from Wilson asked the bankers to reconstitute the consortium.[69] But Bryan's act was consistent with his peace principles and, to say the least, a gesture in the right direction.

Our relations with Japan were embittered by the alien land legislation of California. After the President had failed to persuade the legislature of that state to leave the matter to diplomacy, Bryan somewhat reluctantly went to the coast to see what he could do. The Californians were resentful and in no frame of mind to be advised by federal authorities as to the kind of legislation they should pass. When Bryan attempted to give such advice, the President held him back.[70] But in general he presented the administration's case tactfully, and answered in good part the questions showered at him by the unfriendly legislators who heard him behind closed doors. When asked whether there would be war if the California bill making it impossible for Japanese to own land passed, Bryan replied in the negative, but protested "that the pride of a friendly nation should not be wounded simply because its national debt happened to be large enough to preclude that possibility."[71] Although the legislature refused to incorporate the most important modifications urged by the federal government, it did, thanks to Bryan, make some minor concessions.[72] These, however, were in no way satisfactory to Japan, and the protest she drew up characterized the law as "obnoxious, discriminatory, unfair, unfriendly, and in violation of the treaty." Indeed, relations with Japan became so strained that a crisis was perhaps

[68] Representative Charles Bennett Smith (Democrat, Buffalo) criticized Bryan for not protesting or interfering to prevent the subjugation of China to foreign powers, New York *Times*, Nov. 8, 1915.

[69] Croly, *op. cit.*, 453.

[70] Baker, *op. cit.*, IV, 79-80.

[71] Brooklyn *Eagle*, quoted in the Springfield *Republican*, May 3, 1913.

[72] Springfield *Republican*, May 4, 1913, editorial. The Webb Act did allow a three year lease of land to aliens ineligible for citizenship. New York *Times*, May 3, 1913.

averted when the Secretary of State persuaded the cabinet and the President not to order movements of the Pacific fleet since that might provoke hostilities.[73] Bryan was also authorized to ask the Japanese ambassador to modify the note which seemed certain to arouse great resentment throughout the country as well as in California. When, in a celebrated interview, the Ambassador remarked, "I suppose, Mr. Secretary, this decision is final," Bryan, with an outstretched hand and a winning smile replied, "There is nothing final between friends." Chinda was touched, and the Japanese note was revised.[74] Other factors, to be sure, influenced Japan's decision.[75] But it was to Bryan's credit that he insisted on pacific overtures which, with the full backing of the President, avoided a crisis and perhaps, even, a war.

The President also approved the incorporation in the note of reply to Japan a point Bryan had suggested. Convinced that the problem could be settled by a dispersion of the Japanese in California so as to relieve the economic pressure which had aroused so much opposition there, Bryan had discussed with Chinda a plan by which this might be accomplished. The two governments might coöperate in reducing the number of Japanese in California by one half, encouraging them to go elsewhere, with distribution maintained to prevent similar situations from arising.[76]

The New York *Times* admitted that Bryan's policy of treating "every apparently acute disagreement with a prescription of endless conversation" had worked well. If the matter was unsettled, and a settlement still not in sight, at least the attitude of both countries had changed. The *Times* editorially went on to observe that Bryan acted with a courage which was proof against ridicule —that it was good diplomacy, when everything seemed definitely at an end, to keep on talking about it. If nothing had been settled,

[73] Houston, *op. cit.*, I, 65-67. See *ante.* 168.
[74] *Memoirs*, 367.
[75] Possibly Great Britain used her influence with her ally, Japan, to soften her indignation against the United States. Paxton Hibben, *The Peerless Leader*, 328.
[76] Bryan to Wilson, March 8, 1915, *Letters from Woodrow Wilson;* Baker, *op. cit.*, IV, 83-84.

at least a question full of dynamite had been relegated, for the time at least, to the background, and thirteen months after passion actually threatened a breach, the violence of feeling in both countries had all but disappeared.[77]

Bryan's peace principles were tried and tested in our relations with Haiti, Santo Domingo, Nicaragua, Colombia, and Mexico; and with China and Japan as well. Successful in carrying out his pacifist doctrines in some instances, he failed in others. But all these trials were as nothing in comparison with those presented by the world war. It was as if fate itself had put Bryan, the pacifist, into the office he held when almost the whole world repudiated the method of pacific settlement of disputes and appealed to the sword. Never had a predecessor been more sorely tried; never had a pacifist had such an opportunity to demonstrate the efficacy or the futility of peace principles after war had broken loose. It was to be a contest of epic proportions.

As early as July 28, 1914, Bryan received a cable from Herrick, our ambassador in Paris, expressing the conviction that a strong plea from the President for delay and moderation would meet with the respect and approval of Europe.[78] Bryan at once requested Page in London to inform Grey that the United States stood ready to come forward with a proffer of good offices[79] and renewed the overture. Grey might have accepted our good offices, but refrained. On August 3, Page informed the Secretary of State that there was now not the slightest chance of any result in case our good offices were suggested in any continental capital.[80] In spite of this advice, Bryan the next day instructed our ambassadors in Vienna, Berlin and Russia to deliver in person to the sovereigns an offer of mediation under Article 3 of the Hague Convention, and on August 5 similar instructions were sent to Paris and London.[81] Perhaps no good result would have followed had Bryan

[77] New York *Times*, June 27, 1914.
[78] *Foreign Relations, 1914, Supplement,* 18-19.
[79] *Ibid.*, 29.
[80] *Ibid.*, 37.
[81] *Ibid.*, 42. On July 31, the International Bureau of Peace, which had hastily summoned a gathering of pacifists, cabled Wilson urging him to offer mediation. *Advocate of Peace,* LXXVI, Nov. 1914, 237.

taken action earlier than he did. But the fact that he did not do
so was the result of Page's discouraging cables and the pressure
Colonel House put on the President not to let Bryan make overtures to any of the Powers, since they looked upon him as "absolutely visionary."[82]   A plea to the Powers, when it was first
suggested by Herrick, ought to have been made immediately if
at all; but Bryan trusted to Page, who was presumably better
informed, when he might better have acted on his own pacifist
promptings.

Mediation remained a magic word for Bryan, and nothing
shook his faith that the United States should play the rôle of
peacemaker.   Indeed, everything that happened confirmed this
conviction. The replies of the sovereigns to the offer of mediation
did not discourage him. On receiving the response of the Czar he
wrote to Wilson:

"If you will examine the five answers received, you will be
reminded of that passage in the Scriptures which says that, they
all with one accord began to make excuses. Each one declares he
is opposed to war and anxious to avoid it and then lays the blame
on someone else. The German Ambassador this morning blamed
Russia and congratulated his country that the Emperor did what
he could to avoid war. He also commends the efforts of France
and Great Britain to avoid war, but the Czar is charged with being
the cause."

Bryan suggested that when a way opened to present the matter
of mediation again, quotations be made from the mouths of the
belligerents, all of whom regretted the war and declared their
opposition to it.[83]

The Secretary of State seized every straw which might offer
some chance for mediation. He welcomed warmly a delegation of
leading pacifists who on August 19, 1914, presented a memorial
urging such a course. Expressions of this sort strengthened his
hands.[84]   He played an eager and thoroughly sympathetic rôle

[82] Seymour, *The Intimate Papers of Colonel House*, I, 278-279.
[83] Bryan to Wilson, Aug. 28, 1914. *Bryan Letter Books, Mar. 13, 1913, to Nov. 20, 1914.*
[84] *Advocate of Peace*, LXXVI, Oct. 1914, 204-205.

during the Straus incident in September, 1914: on the strength of
Bernstorff's remark that Germany would be favorable towards
mediation, Bryan cabled the Kaiser. But Berlin's response was
that the Secretary of State should first address himself to the Allies,
since the further course of negotiations depended on their attitude,
which was not yet known.[85] As no encouragement came from
London, the matter was dropped.

But Bryan was indefatigable. He urged the President, on September 19, to offer mediation. On October 13, he cabled the
warring nations a resolution adopted by the Pan-American Union
conveying an earnest expression of its hope for peace.[86] But
Colonel House played into the Allies' hands by persuading the
President to do nothing, and by influencing the administration to
abandon its effort to induce England to accept the Declaration of
London. On August 4, 1915, he stated that had we started
peace parleys in November of the preceding year, we could have
forced "a peace which would eliminate militarism both on land
and sea. The wishes of the Allies were heeded, with the result
that the war has now fastened itself upon the vitals of Europe."[87]
Though fettered, Bryan still did not give up hope of effecting mediation. He urged it openly in a public address in New York on
October 4, 1914.[88] To Carnegie he suggested the advisability of
a personal appeal to the Kaiser—Carnegie had met the German
ruler on several occasions. The philanthropist promised to watch
his opportunity, although he thought America must wait patiently

[85] Straus, Sept. 8, 1914, to Bryan; Straus, Sept. 16, 1914, to Bryan, *Bryan
Papers,* 36; Bernstorff, *My Three Years in America,* 68 ff; Oscar S. Straus,
Under Four Administrations (Boston and New York, 1922), 378-380; Viscount Grey of Fallodon, *Twenty-Five Years,* II, 119-121.
[86] Bryan on August 17, 1914, had suggested that the Pan-American Union
commend Wilson's offer of mediation. Wilson felt that this would do no
harm, and might make for better inter-American relations. Bryan found,
early in October, that suggestions had come from Europe to certain Latin-
American Powers regarding the possibility of mediation. While Bryan
thought we would act with less embarrassment alone, he pointed out that it
would be difficult to refuse other nations that might desire the honor of
joining us. Bryan to Wilson, Oct. 1914, *Bryan Letter Books,* Mar. 13, 1913,
to Nov. 20, 1914. See also *Advocate of Peace,* LXXVI, Nov. 1914, 224.
[87] Seymour, *The Intimate Papers of Colonel House,* II, 61.
[88] New York *Times,* Oct. 5, 1914.

for the exhaustion of one or another party before entering the arena with healing bandages.[89]   Early in January, 1915, Bryan was disappointed in the hope he entertained of going personally to Europe to further mediation: Colonel House had been chosen for that purpose.[90]   But at least he could aid Jane Addams and her associates who, under great difficulties, met with women from other nations at The Hague to promote mediation and prepare for a just and durable peace.[91]   His sympathy with this venture—he went out of his way to help the American women reach their destination—was in marked contrast to Lansing's chilly attitude towards the Ford peace party a year later.   Again and again thereafter Bryan hammered away at the President to try mediation.[92]

Mediation and an early end of the war was not enough: he also wanted a just peace.   On September 19, 1914, he presented to the President a point of view which Wilson finally accepted and acted upon too late:

"The responsibility for continuing the war is just as grave as the responsibility for beginning it, and this responsibility, if pressed upon the consideration of the belligerent nations, might lead them to consent to mediation. . . . The world looks to us to lead the way, and I know your deep desire to render every possible assistance. . . . Both sides seem to entertain the old idea that fear is the only basis upon which peace can rest.   It is not likely that either side will win so complete a victory as to be able to dictate terms, and if either side does win such a victory, it will probably mean preparation for another war.   It would seem better to look for a more rational basis of peace . . . the most potent of all influences for the promotion of peace is the substitution of friendship for hatred. . . . Mediation would give oportunity for the consideration of all

[89] Andrew Carnegie. Oct. 5, 1914, to Bryan, *Bryan Papers*, 36.
[90] Seymour, *The Intimate Papers of Colonel House*, I, 352; II, 18, 19, 21.
[91] *Foreign Relations, 1915, Supplement*, 29, 30, 41, 78.
[92] *Memoirs*, 397.   Bryan stopped short before only one willow-the-wisp opportunity held out to him in the interest of peace.   That was an offer from the New York Peace Society for a million dollars to defray the expenses of a joint commission to be appointed by two neutrals for the purpose of investigating the immediate causes of the European war, and for developing a plan for negotiating a satisfactory settlement.   In submitting the project to the President, he pointed out that such a commission might jeopardize efforts for mediation.   Wilson agreed that his secretary's judgment was sound and discreet.   Bryan to Wilson, Sept. 5, 1914, *Letter Books, Mar. 13, 1913-Nov. 20, 1914.*

plans, and I see no other way in which these plans can be considered or even proposed, for complete success by either side will make that side feel that it is in a position to compel peace by the exercise of superior force."[93]

In spite of all Bryan did to persuade Wilson to offer mediation and promote a rational peace, it was not his fortune to be in office when the President officially called on the belligerents to state their terms, and advocated a just peace without victory. Once more Bryan had forecast a position which another was to take up and make his own. But the peace program which Wilson advanced in December, 1916 and in the following month, similar though it was to Bryan's earlier proposals, came too late to change the pattern of events.[94]

Bryan's greatest contribution to the cause of peace during the war lay in the influence he exerted for the maintenance of true neutrality. In spite of his shortcomings, he was, according to a careful scholar, the only member of the administration who consistently urged a constructive policy for avoiding the dangers that beset its course: his policy offered "the nearest approach to statesmanlike vision and comprehension of realities displayed by any of President Wilson's advisers."[95] He began by informing the President on August 10, 1914, that Morgan and Company had inquired whether there would be any objection to a loan for the French government and the Rothschilds, which, presumably, was also intended for the French government. Bryan had consulted with Assistant Secretary Lansing, who knew of no legal objection to the loan. All precedents, on the contrary, were in favor of such loans. They had not been regarded as a violation of neutrality. But Bryan was not content to follow the legal precedent, particularly when, as in this case, he saw grave dangers in doing so. Money, he observed, was in reality the worst of all contraband, because it commanded everything else. The question of making loans contraband by international agreement had been discussed,

[93] *Memoirs,* 388 ff.
[94] "William Jennings Bryan" in *American Secretaries of State,* X, 33.
[95] *Ibid.,* 31.

but no action had been taken. "I know of nothing," continued Bryan in his letter to Wilson, "that would do more to prevent war than an international agreement that neutral nations would not loan to belligerents."[96] Could we not hasten such an agreement by refusing to approve of any loans to a belligerent? Such a refusal, he insisted, would tend to hasten the conclusion of the war. The only way of testing our influence was, after all, that of example. In addition, Bryan pointed out another objection to the customary practice of neutral loans to belligerents. A loan to a Power would be taken as an expression of sympathy; and if loans were made to all the belligerents, our citizens would be divided into groups, each lending to the country it favored. Even more astute was his observation that

"the powerful financial interests which would be connected with these loans would be tempted to use their influence through the newspapers to support the interests of the Government to which they had loaned because the value of the security would be directly affected by the result of the war. We would thus find our newspapers violently arrayed on the one side or the other, each paper supporting a financial group and a pecuniary interest. All of this influence would make it all the more difficult for us to maintain neutrality, as our action on various questions that would arise would affect one side or the other and powerful financial interests would be thrown into the balance."[97]

Agreeing with his chief, Lansing had contributed a further argument to fortify his position. Our citizens, he observed, who went abroad and enlisted, lost the protection of their citizenship while so engaged. There was no reason for giving greater protection to American dollars which went abroad and enlisted in the cause of a belligerent. While our government could not prevent either men or dollars from going abroad at their own risk, its influence was used to prevent men from doing so. Why should its influence not be used to prevent dollars from doing so?

A day or two after Bryan wrote this letter to Wilson, he conferred with him on this question at the White House. The

[96] Bryan to Wilson, August 10, 1914. *Bryan Papers*, 36.
[97] *Ibid.*

President approved his proposition not to sanction loans to belligerents, and at his suggestion, wrote a sentence stating that position strongly and concisely. Bryan incorporated it in the statement he made on August 15 to the effect that loans by American bankers to any belligerent nation were inconsistent with the true spirit of neutrality.[98] This was, apparently, the first time that any great nation had taken such a position. Unofficial peace congresses had spoken their approval,[99] and Bryan himself in 1907 had sponsored this plan at the great national peace congress in New York.[100] He was right in regarding the position his government now took as setting a new standard. However, loans were made to belligerents, in spite of the government's statement which was emasculated by interpretations of legal experts in the state department. On March 31, 1915, while Bryan was still secretary of state, and without his protest, an announcement was made to the effect that the government did not feel justified in objecting to the credit arrangements made privately by banks.[101] This was the natural and inevitable procedure in a capitalistic state: bankers were not to be expected to put patriotism before profits, nor was the government able or willing to put pressure on them to do so. Bryan's head was in the right place, but he could not keep it there without repudiating capitalism itself. His prediction, however, that loans to the belligerents would commit us to their cause proved to be only too true in the judgment of many who later reflected on these events.

Defeated on the question of financial neutrality, Bryan also fought a losing battle for the maintenance of an impartial commercial attitude towards the belligerents.[102] On August 6, 1914,

[98] *Memoirs*, 375-376. *Foreign Relations, 1914, Supplement,* 580, the Secretary of State to J. P. Morgan and Company, Aug. 15, 1914. The statement said that there was no reason for not making loans to the governments of neutral nations; *Ibid., 1915, Supplement,* 820.

[99] M. E. Curti, *The American Peace Crusade, 1815-1861* (Durham, N. C., 1929), 176, 181.

[100] *Ante.* 141.

[101] Seymour, *The Intimate Papers of Colonel House,* II, 70.

[102] True, Bryan did win some minor victories for the maintenance of our neutrality. Officials in the state department proposed a protest against

he proposed that the Declaration of London be accepted for the governance of the combatants on the seas. Had his proposal been recognized, neutral rights would have enjoyed certain protections. Germany and Austria, who also stood to gain from its recognition, agreed to accept the Declaration; Great Britain, who had refused to accept it in peace time, had no intention of doing so now. Page thought Bryan made his first great mistake in asking England to accept it, since acceptance was regarded in London as tantamount to losing the war.[103] Actually, he was probably wise in trying to avoid, in advance, the infractions on our neutral rights which resulted in so much acrimony, and, finally our entrance into the war. He was, indeed, not mistaken in proposing the acceptance of the Declaration of London: his mistake was his failure to use as a lever our control of materials which were indispensable to the Allies.[104] But it is doubtful whether this could have been done in a society in which profit was the keynote. Our sale of material to the Allies not only established a favorable economic situation for us; it actually brought our makers of munition and of a thousand other things, as well as our food producers, unprecedented profits. Bryan's limitation in not using as a lever our control of necessities to wring concessions from the Allies was simply the limitation of the dominant economic system which he accepted and in which the vast majority of fellow-Americans likewise believed. His political forefather, Thomas Jefferson, had, indeed, experimented under somewhat parallel conditions with an embargo; but that had failed even when the industrial and commercial element in the

Germany's use of airships for bombardments, but the Secretary put his foot down. "I am so anxious," he wrote to the President on August 29, 1914, "that we shall avoid anything that can possibly bring us into collision with the belligerent powers that I am not sure that we should make any protest at all. The same caution which leads me to doubt whether we should make any protest naturally leads me to favor the one least likely to raise objection. . . . There being no international provision which is clearly violated, we would not, I think, be justified in making protest simply on humanitarian grounds." Bryan to Wilson, Aug. 29, 1914, *Bryan Papers*, 36.

[103] Burton J. Hendrick, *The Life and Letters of Walter Hines Page*, I, 373, 377.

[104] "William Jennings Bryan," in *American Secretaries of States*, X, 24-25.

population was far less influential, proportionately to the agricul-
tural, than was now the case.

But even within the limitations imposed by our economic system of production for profit, Bryan did not play his cards as
effectively as he might have done. Both Page and Spring-Rice,
the British ambassador in Washington, insisted that war might
result if we pushed England too far towards an acceptance of the
principles of the Declaration of London; and Wilson and House
shared that fear. It was Bryan's pacifism which, ironically, led
him to share it too. He did not want a war with England; and
he was led to accept the concessions which were arranged, during
his absence on political work, by his Assistant Secretary, Lansing,
and by legal experts in the department. He might have realized
that England would be loath and indeed foolish to add to her foes
a country which would provide her with indispensable materials,
even if her enemy did get half the loaf. To what extent his
reliance on moral force, or his absence during the negotiations,
or his pacific willingness to compromise in order to prevent danger
of war, led him to take the course he took, we cannot be certain.
It is now clear that in doing so he was not solving any fundamental
problem. The concessions to Great Britain given in the winter of
1914 and the spring of 1915 did not end either her infractions on
our neutral rights, or friction between the two countries. But
these concessions did pave the way for German retaliations which
even more dramatically encroached on our neutral rights. Had
Bryan insisted on maintaining a firm position towards Great
Britain from the first, he might have had to resign. But such a
course, difficult though it may have been would have been consistent with his principles and would have promised the most for
their realization.

As a result of the conciliatory and in a sense unneutral policy
to which Bryan assented, the Allies throttled the import trade of
Germany and practically monopolized our exports.[105] The Secretary of State was the first and the most persistent member of the

[105] *American Secretaries of State*, X, 29-30.

administration to point out that our policy might well lead Germany, despairing of relief through our own insistence on Britain's respect for our neutral rights, to take desperate measures—measures which might involve us in a war with her. On February 4, 1915, Berlin gave notice of a submarine warfare which threatened to involve the destruction of American vessels and lives inasmuch as England covered her ships with neutral flags to insure their immunity from attack.[106] Bryan signed the strong protest which warned Germany that we should hold her responsible for the loss of American lives or ships by the new submarine policy. Hoping for some way which would lead to a compromise, he wrote to the President on February 5, 1915, in regard to the pressing food situation in Germany which had led to the new policy of unrestricted submarine warfare in the war zone surrounding the British Isles:

"The situation is growing more and more delicate and under the proposed war zone plan we are liable, at any time, to have a disaster over there which will inflame public opinion—and we are not in a position to meet this outburst of public opinion unless we have done all that we can to prevent it. I am led to believe from conversations with the German and Austrian ambassadors that there would be a chance of securing the withdrawal of the military zone order in return for favorable action on the food question. I do not know in what direction your mind is moving on the subject but I feel myself more and more inclined to the opinion that the British position is without justification. The German government is willing to give assurances that food imported will not be taken by the Government, and is even willing that American organizations shall distribute that food. This, it seems to me, takes away the British excuse for attempting to prevent the importation of food. You will notice in the last note the bitterness of tone in which the German Government speaks of the attempts to starve non-combatants. If I am not mistaken the efforts to bring this 'economic pressure' as they call it, upon women and children of Germany will offend the moral sense of our country, and, of course, still further arouse those who are inclined to sympathize with Germany. I am constrained to believe that it is worth while for us to make an attempt to adjust the difficulty by setting one of these propositions off against the other. I mean

[106] Bryan also at this time signed a protest to England against the use of our flag to cover her ships, but this protest was ineffective.

that we should see whether Great Britain will not withdraw her objection to food entering Germany—the same to be distributed there through American instrumentalities, in return for the withdrawal of the German order in regard to the war zone. . . If we cannot thus clear the atmosphere I believe that we are approaching the most serious crisis that we have had to meet."[107]

Wilson approved of Bryan's suggestion, and on February 20 identical notes were sent to England and Germany proposing such a reciprocal arrangement.[108] But Page reported that he did not see a ray of hope for this proposal.[109] Germany seemed inclined with certain qualifications to accept[110] a modified use of mines and submarines in return for American exports, particularly if the United States would agree to put an embargo on arms and munitions to the Allies unless they also accepted the proposition. Bryan refused to do this.[111] He had, in a letter to Senator Stone, chairman of the committee on foreign relations, maintained, only a month earlier, that interference with the sending of munitions to the Allies was unwarranted and unneutral.[112] True, he realized that, while the sale of munitions could not be forbidden, it had worked so entirely for the benefit of the Allies as to give Germany, not justification, but an excuse for claiming that we were favoring the Allies.[113] Certainly an embargo on munitions would have led the Allies to charge us with unneutral discriminations—and it would have cut into the revenues of a substantial American business. It would, of course, have been impossible for the Allies to have drawn munitions from America had our government possessed a monopoly of the business, as Bryan believed it should. Yet he did

[107] Bryan to Wilson, Feb. 15, 1915; Bryan to Wilson, Feb. 19, 1915, *Bryan Papers*, 36.

[108] *Foreign Relations, 1915,* 111, 120.

[109] *Ibid.,* 118-119, 122, 125.

[110] *Ibid.,* Gerard to Bryan, Feb. 24, 1915, 123, 126.

[111] *Ibid.,* 129.

[112] *Ibid., 1914, Supplement,* xiv. Bryan to Stone, Jan. 20, 1915. "If Germany and Austria cannot import contraband from this country, it is not, because of that fact, the duty of the United States to close its markets to the Allies. The markets of this country are open upon equal terms to all the world, to every nation, belligerent or neutral." This, of course, was true in theory, but by virtue of the effective British blockade, untrue in fact.

[113] *Memoirs,* 397.

not now, in this connection, urge that point. The fact was also overlooked that the Secretary of State had not regarded an embargo on arms for Mexico as either unwarranted or unneutral. Even if it was a perfectly neutral act for us to send munitions to the Allies, the fact could not be dodged that it meant a prolongation of the war.

Nevertheless Bryan did not mean to let the tide of events push us into the war. When Thrasher, an American passenger on a British steamer, was drowned, he disagreed with the position of the President, who proposed a note which seemed certain to inflame the already hostile feeling against us in Germany. Bryan pointed out that our attitude towards the two belligerents was in marked contrast. If we admitted the right of the submarine to attack merchantmen but condemned their particular act or class of acts as inhuman, then we should be embarrassed by the fact that we had not protested against England's defense of the right to prevent foods from reaching noncombatant enemies.[114]   In returning to the President letters from O'Laughlin and Muensterberg, Bryan stated his position in a letter dated April 19, 1915:

"There is no doubt as to the sentiment in Germany and the view they take is a natural one. 1st. They have warned Americans not to travel on British ships. Why do Americans take the risk? This was not an unreasonable question. 2d. If we allowed the use of our flag, how can we complain, if in the confusion one of our boats is sunk by mistake? 3rd. Why be shocked at the drowning of a few people, if there is no objection to the starving of a nation? Of course Germany insists that by careful use she will have food enough, but if Great Britain cannot succeed in starving the non-combatants, why does she excite retaliation by threatening to do so? If we are to prove our neutrality—and unless we do—we are likely to be drawn into the conflict by the growing feeling in Germany—it seems to me we must prevent the misuse of our flag and warn Americans not to use British vessels in the war zone unless we can bring pressure on Great Britain to withdraw the threat to make bread or food contraband. Our identical note was well intended and Germany indicated a willingness to negotiate. . . . Would it not be wise to make another effort to persuade Great Britain to join in some agreement which will, by permitting food

[114] *Ibid.,* 396.

to go into Germany, do away with torpedoing of merchant vessels? Otherwise, the continued export of arms is likely to get us into trouble. So much for the O'Laughlin letter.

"The Muensterberg letter indicates that Germany is ready for peace. I doubt if the terms he proposes are possible. I doubt if it is possible to propose terms, but I feel and have felt for some time that we should urge the Allies to consent to a conference at which terms shall be discussed. It is impossible for either side to annihilate the other, and a continuance of the struggle . . . adds to the horrors . . . and endangers neutrals.[115]

"The loss of one American, who might have avoided death, is as nothing compared with the tens of thousands who are daily dying in this 'causeless war'. Is it not better to try to bring peace for the benefit of the whole world than to risk the provoking of war on account of one man?"[116]

On April 27, Wilson told Bryan at a meeting of the cabinet that he was not at all confident that he was on the right track in having instructed Lansing to draw up the protest he outlined to Germany. On the next day, writing to the Secretary of State, the President admitted that Bryan's letter had "made a deep impression." He went so far as to say that possibly it was not necessary "to make formal representations in the matter at all." Indeed, as a result of Bryan's influence, no communication was sent to Berlin. But he could not accept Bryan's alternative—a public call upon the belligerents to end the war.

"I wish I could see it as you do. But in view of what House writes I cannot. It is known to every government concerned that we believe the war should be ended and that we speak for all neutral nations in that wish. It is known that we are seeking to help— that anything they want to say to each other, they can say through us. At present they are most appreciative and cordial. . . . We know their minds and we know their difficulties. They are dependent on their own public opinion (even Germany) and we know what this is . . . we would lose such influence as we have for peace."[117] . . . "there are no terms of peace spoken of (at any

[115] Bryan to Wilson, Apr. 19, 1915, *Bryan Papers, Woodrow Wilson Letters*.

[116] Bryan to Wilson, Apr. 23, 1915. Only part of this letter is included in the *Memoirs*, 396-397.

[117] Wilson to Bryan, Apr. 28, 1915, *Bryan Papers, Woodrow Wilson Letters*.

rate in Germany) which are not so selfish and impossible that
the other side are ready to resist them to their last man and
dollar. . . . Reasonableness has not yet been burned into them,
and what they are thinking of is, not the peace and prosperity of
Europe, but their own aggrandizement, an impossible modern
basis (it might be well for Japan to reflect) for peace."[118]

Thus the situation stood when, on May 7, news came of the
loss of American lives by the sinking of the *Lusitania*. Bryan at
once called the attention of the President to the fact that the
Lusitania carried ammunition, and urged that ships bearing contraband be forbidden to carry passengers.[119] Germany had a right to
prevent contraband from going to the Allies, "and a ship carrying
contraband should not rely upon passengers to protect her from
attack—it would be like putting women and children in front of
an army."

Wilson, unmoved by Bryan's argument, himself prepared a
note to Germany which was discussed in cabinet meeting on May
11. When Bryan objected that it would mean war, the President
consented to consider the problem further. The next day Bryan
received drafts from the President and from Lansing. Since the
words used by the President were less harsh than those of Lansing,
the Secretary of State preferred those of his chief.[120] In looking
over the last sentence of this first *Lusitania* note, Bryan observed
that there was no concluding reiteration of our friendship for
Germany. Lansing thought such a sentence unnecessary, and Wilson agreed with him.[121] The Secretary of State regretted this
decision, because he feared that the Jingoes would assume that the
note meant war, an interpretation which might affect the tone of
Germany's reply and render it harder to postpone final settlement.
He therefore proposed to the President that a statement be made
to the effect that the words "strict accountability" did not mean,
as some newspaper men insisted, an immediate settlement of the
matter. Sometimes individual friends found it wise to postpone

[118] Wilson to Bryan, Apr. 28, 1915, *Bryan Letter Book*.
[119] *Memoirs*, 398-399.
[120] Bryan to Wilson, May 12, 1915, *Bryan Letter Book*.
[121] Bryan to Wilson, May 13, 1915, *ibid*.

the settlement of disputes until they could be calmly considered on their merits; and such ought to be the case with nations. Germany had endorsed the principle of investigation embodied in the thirty treaties, and there was no reason why delay and investigation should not now be utilized.[122] Wilson, after sleeping over the suggestion, agreed in part, and prepared a typewritten memorandum which was to be given out to the press from the Executive Office as a "tip" at the time when the note was published. The memorandum[123] expressed the confidence of the administration in an accommodating response from Germany, referred to the principle of deliberation and inquiry embodied in the Bryan treaties, and stated that it was believed Germany would also act in the same spirit. But the memorandum was not given out to the press. Having learned something indirectly from the German embassy which convinced him that such a statement would forfeit all chance of bringing Germany to reason, Wilson did not release it.[124] In reply to Bryan's note expressing regret that he had changed his mind, the President replied:

"I was as sorry as you could have been to withdraw the 'statement' which we had intended for the press. It cost me a struggle to do so. But the intimation was plain from the German Embassy (and I cannot doubt the source of information) that we were not in earnest, and would speak only in a Pickwickian sense if we seemed to speak with firmness, and I did not dare lend color to that impression. You will notice that the hope of a pacific settlement was expressed. That, in the circumstances, was as far as I dared to go."[125]

Bryan joined in sending the protest to Germany "with a heavy

[122] *Memoirs*, 399-400.
[123] *Ibid.,* 400-401.
[124] *Ibid.,* 401-402.
[125] Wilson to Bryan, May 14, 1915, *Bryan Letter Book*. See also David Lawrence, *The True Story of Woodrow Wilson*, 144 ff. In the campaign of 1916 the secret of the proposed memorandum postponing the reckoning leaked out in a garbled form. In his statement to Walter Lippmann the President said that no postscript or amendment to the note was ever written or contemplated by himself except changes which strengthened or emphasized the protest. He admitted that one member of the Cabinet spoke to him about a supplementary softening instruction, but that he had rejected the suggestion.

heart." He signed it, not because he agreed, "but because it was the opening statement of our position and simply called for a similar statement on the part of Germany."[126]   He thought the President could not have stated his opinion more clearly and effectively, and contented himself with offering a few suggestions. The wording he would change here and there. He would make some reference to the German offer to apologize and make reparation in case a neutral ship were sunk by a mistake. He would point out that while an apology and reparation might satisfy international obligation, if no loss of life resulted, it could not justify or excuse a practice, the natural and almost necessary effect of which was to subject neutrals to new and innumerable risks, since peace, not war, was the normal state, and nations resorting to war were not at liberty to subordinate the rights of neutrals to the supposed or even the actual needs of belligerents. Bryan was sure of Wilson's patriotic purpose, but he could not relinquish his belief that the wise course was to play the rôle of friend to both parties by acting as peacemaker: this note, he feared, would result in the relinquishment of that rôle. It would, to be sure, be popular in the United States, for a time at least, perhaps permanently; public sentiment, already favorable to the Allies, had been made perceptibly more so by the *Lusitania* tragedy. But in that very fact there was peril: "Your position being that of the government, will be approved, the approval varying according to the intensity of feeling against Germany. There being no intimation that the final accounting will be postponed until the war is over, the jingo element will not only predict but demand war." The Washington *Post* editorially was already taking that position; and now this note would have the effect of drawing more distinctly the line between those who sympathize with Germany and the rest of the people. Abroad, the Allies would of course applaud, and the more they applauded, the more embittered Germany would become. Naturally, too; for while we denounced her methods we did not complain about the announced intention of the Allies to starve noncombatant Germany and to use passenger ships carrying American citizens to give im-

[126] *Memoirs*, 421.

munity to vessels with munitions of war, without even the care bestowed on ships carrying horses and gasoline. On top of that, Great Britain increasingly showed indifference toward the misuse of our flag and toward unwarranted interference with our trade with neutrals. Germany could not but construe as partiality the strong case made by our note against her, while we kept silent about Allied conduct. Would Wilson not consent to issue simultaneously a statement about the objectionable behavior of England and France, which would keep them from rejoicing and which would show Germany that we were defending our rights against aggression from both sides?[127]

While the President was willing to consider this, he would not listen to Bryan's plea for an official warning to Americans not to take passage on belligerent vessels carrying contraband. On May 14, the day after the first *Lusitania* note was sent, the President informed him that to issue such a warning would be telling Germany that we did not mean all we said when we stated we meant to support our citizens in the exercise of their rights to travel both on our ships and on those of the belligerents. Bryan's suggestion he deemed weak and futile.[128]

Thus while Bryan's influence somewhat moderated the first *Lusitania* note, he was defeated in all that he deemed most essential: passengers were not to be warned; the supplementary memorandum to the press suggesting that we would debate the issue in a friendly spirit was not issued; and though Bryan was permitted to work on a protest to England the note was made to wait on the negotiations of Colonel House.

Bryan forwarded to the President a draft of the protest to Great Britain which Lansing had drawn up. The President, upon learning from House that England would now consider the American proposal of February 22 to abandon the food blockade if Germany would give up submarine attacks on merchant vessels, determined to hold up the protest to England until Germany had

[127] Bryan to Wilson, (undated, but probably May 13, 1915), *Bryan Papers.*
[128] *Memoirs,* 403; Wilson to Bryan, May 14, 1915, *Bryan Letter Book.*

answered our note on the sinking of the *Lusitania*. In informing Bryan of his decision on May 20, Wilson wrote:

". . . we cannot afford even to seem to be trying to make it easier for Germany to accede to our demands by turning in similar fashion to England concerning matters which we have already told Germany are none of her business. It would be so evident a case of uneasiness and hedging that I think it would weaken our whole position fatally. . . . In every such decision I feel very keenly the force of your counter judgment and cannot claim that I feel cocksure of the rightness of my own conclusions; but I can only follow what grows more and more clear to me the more I think the matter out."[129]

Had England and Germany been able to agree on abandoning reciprocally the food blockade and submarine warfare, our case against both nations would probably have been closed.[130] But Germany insisted that raw materials be admitted as well as food; and to this Britain would not consent.[131] The failure of this effort to remove the causes of Germany's violations of our neutral rights doubtless made her reply of May 28 to our *Lusitania* note less satisfactory than it might otherwise have been.

Although Bryan was not responsible for the German refusal to accept the British offer, House and Gerard insisted that certain of his actions made Germany less ready to accept a compromise, both in that instance, and in her reply of May 28 to our *Lusitania* protest—a reply in which, they thought, she not only refused to meet our demands, but tried to justify the sinking of the *Lusitania*. They had in mind the so-called Dumba incident. After an interview with Bryan on May 17, the Austrian ambassador, Dr. Dumba, had sent the following message by radio, via Berlin, to the Austrian minister of foreign affairs:

"The United States desires no war. Her Notes, however strongly worded, meant no harm, but had to be written in order to pacify public opinion of America. The Berlin Government therefore need not feel itself injured, but need only make suitable concessions if it desires to put an end to the dispute."[132]

[129] Wilson to Bryan, May 20, 1915, *Bryan Letter Book.*
[130] *Ibid.*, House to Wilson, London, May 21, 1915.
[131] *Ibid.*, Wilson to Bryan, May 23, 1915.
[132] Bernstorff, *My Three Years in America*, 155.

Just what Bryan said in his interview with Dumba can never be exactly ascertained, for there was no dictaphone in the office of the Secretary of State. There was doubtless a mutual misunderstanding as to what was said and meant. On the one hand, Bryan was deeply agitated during these days, anxious to prevent war, disappointed in the harshness of the *Lusitania* note, and, at the same time, apt to be confiding and trusting. Although Dumba's cable, partly by virtue of its condensation, probably expanded the conciliatory remarks Bryan made, Dumba was too astute a diplomat to have invented his impression out of whole cloth.[133] The Secretary of State also gave his colleague, Houston, the impression that he would be willing to tell Germany that we did not mean anything by our first note if that were necessary to avoid trouble.[134] On the other hand, Bryan on the very day of the interview wrote a letter to the President in which he summarized his conversation with Dumba. This summary, at once accepted by Dumba, and agreeing with the account of the conversation in the memoirs of the Austrian diplomat, was approved by Wilson.[135] There was only one point in this report of the conversation which could have given Dumba the notion that we had not meant what we had said in our first *Lusitania* note. That was Bryan's remark that Dumba might tell Germany that he felt sure there was no desire in America for a war, and that Germany was expected to answer the note in the same spirit of friendship which had prompted the American note. Dumba's cable should have conveyed Bryan's insistence that the German agreement to cease ruthless submarine warfare must be unconditional and not made to depend upon a strong American protest against the English blockade. It should also have conveyed the Secretary of State's emphasis on the "boundless indignation" aroused in America by the terrible deaths of so many American citizens. It may be said in

[133] Robert Lansing, "The Difficulties of Neutrality," *Saturday Evening Post*, Apr. 18, 1931, 6 ff, 101-102.
[134] Houston, *Eight Years with Wilson's Cabinet*, I, 139.
[135] New York *Times*, May 19, 1916 (speech of Bryan at Lake Mohonk); *Memoirs*, 377, 380; Constantin Dumba, *Memoirs of a Diplomat* (Boston, 1932), 232 ff.

Dumba's defence that, only a few days before, he had informed Berlin that a repetition of the *Lusitania* affair would mean war.[136]

Owing to the difficulties of transmission, Dumba's cable to Vienna was known in the German foreign office before it reached the Austrian minister of foreign affairs. Zimmermann, the German assistant secretary of state, committed the indiscretion of reading Dumba's cable, which had not even been addressed to him, to Gerard when he tried to give added weight to the *Lusitania* protest by making sleeping car reservations for himself and family as if a break in diplomatic relations were imminent. Gerard immediately informed House, and thus Wilson, of Dumba's cable. It was then that Bryan sent for Dumba, who expressed surprise that such a misconstruction could have been put on his language, and, at Bryan's request, cabled the German government correcting any such misconstruction. On May 24, Bryan himself cabled Gerard the memorandum he had made of his interview with Dumba, together with that diplomat's approval of its correctness.[137]

House, Gerard and Lansing all believed that Dumba's message, inspired by something Bryan had told him in their interview, was responsible for the uncompromising attitude of the German foreign office in the fourth week of May, 1915. Lansing went so far as to say that Bryan's indiscreet conduct defeated the very purpose of the demands that had been made on Germany and jeopardized the peace he was so anxious to preserve.[138] Gerard thought that Dumba's message had misinformed the German authorities as to the real intention of the President, and that Bryan would be responsible if trouble with Germany broke out.[139] Colonel House also believed that the Dumba incident was responsible for the German refusal to accept his compromise suggestion that in return for the admission of food, but not raw products, the submarine campaign would be abandoned.[140] But these opinions were not

[136] Dumba, *op. cit.*, 235; *Memoirs of William Jennings Bryan*, 377 ff.

[137] *Memoirs of William Jennings Bryan*, 378; *Foreign Relations, 1915, Supplement*, 408; Dumba, *loc. cit.*, 234-235.

[138] Robert Lansing, "The Difficulties of Neutrality," *loc. cit.*, 6 ff., 102.

[139] Seymour, *The Intimate Papers of Colonel House*, II, 26.

[140] *Ibid.*, I, 451, II, 6-7.

entirely justified.[141]   Gerard presented the compromise suggestion
of House to von Jagow immediately on receiving it, May 18.   The
Dumba interview had taken place only the day before.   While
Dumba's cable may conceivably have influenced Germany's refusal
to accept the House compromise,[142] it could not have played a very
large part in the unconciliatory reply to the *Lusitania* note.   It is
certain that Bryan's repudiation of the Dumba note was known
several days in Berlin before the dispatch of the unsatisfactory
reply of May 28 to the *Lusitania* note.   Moreover, Dumba himself
had cabled the German foreign office that a repetition of the torpedoing of a passenger ship without warning meant war with the
United States.   These facts lend support to Wilson's assurance to
Bryan that he did not think him at fault for the interpretation
placed on the Dumba interview in Berlin, and that, in any case,
the incident could not have affected the German attitude in view
of the promptness with which the Secretary of State corrected the
German misapprehension of our attitude.[143]   Nevertheless Bryan
suffered a good deal from the garbled and downright abusive attacks in the Republican and pro-Ally press, colored as they were
with gross exaggerations.[144]

The German note of May 28 on the *Lusitania* led Wilson to
prepare a reply which categorically renewed the demands that had
been made earlier; dismissed the German contentions as irrelevant;

[141] Hilary A. Herbert, secretary of the navy under Cleveland, also thought
that Bryan was responsible for creating the impression in Germany that
American opinion on the *Lusitania* was divided.   Many German newspapers,
he pointed out, urged Germany to make no apologies and no concessions.
When Germany did make concessions, it was because the American press
had demonstrated that American opinion was substantially unanimous.   New
York *Times,* Nov. 21, 1915.

[142] *Foreign Relations, 1915, Supplement,* 415; Bernstorff, *op. cit.,* 156.

[143] Tumulty to Bryan, Dec. 11, 1917, Bryan to Tumulty, Dec. 13, 1917, and
Wilson to Bryan, Dec. 17, 1915, *Bryan Papers, Woodrow Wilson Letter
Book.*

[144] New York *Times,* July 15, 1915.   The New York *Times,* without much
evidence, editorially expressed the opinion that there was an "inherent
probability" in a very garbled version of the story put forward by the
Providence *Journal,* and concluded that Bryan had been so dangerous a
secretary of state that no one could say into what perils he would have
brought the country had he continued.   New York *Times,* July 4, 1915, Nov.
2, May 19, 1916.   See also Dumba, *op. cit.,* 235-236.

and emphasized considerations of humanity. On June 1, at a dramatic meeting of the cabinet, the note was laid on the table for discussion. Bryan, who had obviously been laboring under great strain, observed that he had all along insisted on a note to England, since she was illegally preventing our exports from going where we had a right to send them. Were we to ask the English authorities what we might do and what we might not do? With a "show of heat," the Secretary of State remarked that the cabinet seemed pro-Ally. When the President rebuked him, he apologized.[145] But he pointed out that as the note stood, it left Germany no chance of doing anything but refusing to discontinue submarine warfare. It would be her turn to make the next move; we were placing in her hands the power to declare war, rather than keeping that power in our own hands.[146] After the meeting, he told the President that he could not sign the note. He went home with bloodshot eyes and weary steps. He had been unable to sleep for many nights; and more sleepless nights were ahead of him.[147]

Yet there was some hope that he might be able to have the note modified in such a way as to give Germany a chance to express a willingness for investigation of the facts. The next day, two notes held out encouragement. One came from an official in the state department, W. B. Fleming, which gave him moral support for his position.[148] The other came from the President:

"Will you be kind enough to let me have, for the guidance of my thought on this anxious matter, an outline of the answer you think we should make to the German reply to our note? I feel that I very much need all the counsel that I can get, and I shall, of course, chiefly value yours. I meant to ask you this yesterday."[149]

Responding the same day, June 2, to Wilson's "generous request for suggestions" Bryan urged that an immediate answer to

[145] Houston, *Eight Years in Wilson's Cabinet,* I, 137-138, 139.
[146] *Memoirs,* 422.
[147] William G. McAdoo, *Crowded Years* (Boston and N. Y., 1931), 333.
[148] W. B. Fleming to Bryan (Personal), June 2, 1915, *Bryan Papers,* 36.
[149] Wilson to Bryan, June 2, 1915, *Bryan Papers, Wilson Letter Book.* The President also requested a similar memorandum from Lansing.

Germany should not be made. A wise response was more necessary than a speedy one, and time was a factor of no mean importance. Apparently neither party desired war; and there was always a hope of amicable adjustment when neither side wanted to fight. Our peace plan emphasized the advantages to be gained by deliberation and investigation. The note, he suggested, should be subjected to legal treatment: distinctions should be drawn as in a court, between material and immaterial propositions. But the Secretary of State did not stop with these general suggestions. Point by point and even word by word he proceeded to criticize the memorandum drawn up by Lansing for Wilson's guidance in preparing the note. He was, for example, unable to agree with the Assistant Secretary of State as to the propriety of using, in characterizing vessels, the word "unresisting" instead of "unarmed." The character of a vessel, he pointed out, was determined not by the fact of whether or not she resisted, but whether or not she was armed: if the word "unresisting" were used, the attacking party would not be entitled to employ force until after the vessel had actually used her arms, which would give the vessel attacked great advantage over the one attacking. Neither did Bryan agree with Lansing as to the advisability of requiring the German government to commit itself to the principles involved before the facts of the particular case were discussed: it was the custom of the state department to investigate the facts before taking a position, and there was no reason for refusing the German suggestion that the question of facts be first considered. Bernstorff in conversation had made it clear that the question of fact had been raised in order to give the foreign office a plausible excuse for accepting our proposition if the grounds upon which its action was based proved to be erroneous. If Germany was really looking for a way out, Bryan continued, we could not do otherwise than assist her. This might not be to the advantage of our sensational newspapers, but it would certainly have the approval of the country. Hence, concluded the Secretary of State, let us hold off from sending an immediate reply.[150]

[150] Bryan to Wilson, June 2, 1915, *Bryan Letter Book.*

But the President could not agree, though he politely thanked Bryan for his suggestions and asked him to be good enough to send any further ones that he had. However, on the essential points, he was firm:

"I think that time (though of course not haste) is of the essence in this matter in order that the German Government should be made to feel that we regard it as pressing; for they show not the slightest inclination or purpose to change their methods even pending the interchange of views. . . . It is interesting and significant how often the German Foreign Office goes over the same ground in different words, and always misses the essential point involved, that England's violation of neutral rights is different from Germany's violation of the rights of humanity."[151]

In spite of these dampening notes, Bryan took the President at his word, and on the next day, June 3, made further suggestions regarding the drafting of the *Lusitania* note. After reviewing the cases of the *Cushing,* the *Gulflight* and the *Fabala,* Bryan reiterated more forcibly the position he had previously taken. We could not well object to arbitration where arbitration was possible. Neither could we, in any case, object to investigation since our thirty treaties committed us to that *in all cases* and since this form of treaty was offered to Germany, and in principle accepted by her:

"We cannot consistently refuse to apply this document to all questions that may arise between us. It seems to me that these treaties not only furnish us the most plausible excuse that we can find for investigation, but leave us no valid excuse for not resorting to the plan. Nothing could more forcibly emphasize the value of this peace plan than the employment of it in this case, and now that we have stated our position and received Germany's reply, the objection urged against making the settlement at the time the note was sent would not seem to apply. The use of this idea at this time might even exert a profound influence upon the making of the treaty between belligerent nations at the end of the war. The plan for the investigation of all difficulties is the simplest plan that can he found for dealing with disputed questions and, though simple, gives the greatest promise of effectiveness."[152]

[151] Wilson to Bryan, June 2, 1915, *ibid.*
[152] Bryan to Wilson, Morning, June 3, 1915, *Bryan Letter Book.*

At the same time the Secretary of State recognized the fact that the responsibility was on Wilson's shoulders, and that in the final decision his judgment and conscience could be his only guide. But he had given his chief the advice he would wish to be given were he himself in the position of responsibility—the plan on which he would act.[153] Other brief notes from Bryan kept reminding the President of his solicitude and earnestness in the matter. When, on the evening of June 3, he sent to Wilson the memorandum prepared by Lansing, he pointed out that he did not share with the Assistant Secretary the view that we could entirely ignore the question raised as to whether our law forbidding the carrying of passengers on vehicles bearing ammunition was violated.[154]

Until the mind of the President was completely made up, there was always the chance that he might be moved. Bryan wrote him on June 4 of a visit from Senator Martin of Virginia and Congressman Henry D. Flood, who wanted the President to know that the country did not desire war with Germany. Flood and Martin had talked with other congressmen and senators, and both were certain that they would vote against a declaration of war if the issue were presented. They thought that the *Lusitania* did not justify a resort to hostilities and felt certain that the country did not regard the matter as one which would justify war.[155] The President admitted that the views of Senator Martin and Representative Flood had "made a deep impression" on him. He had no doubt that these views echoed "a great part of public opinion," and wished with all his heart that he saw a way "to carry out the double wish of our people, to maintain a firm front in respect of what we demand of Germany and yet do nothing that might by any possibility involve us in the war."[156]

One of the most interesting pleas Bryan made was that contained in his letter of June 5. Although he had no new points to make, he made the old ones with such convincing sincerity that the letter deserves to be quoted:

[153] Bryan to Wilson, Morning, June 3, 1915, *ibid.*
[154] Bryan to Wilson, June 3, *ibid.*
[155] Bryan to Wilson, June 4, 1915, *ibid.*
[156] *Ibid.*, Wilson to Bryan, June 7, 1915.

"The fact that the note to Germany has not yet been completed encourages me to trespass upon your time for a moment to present again three matters which, to my mind, are necessary to insure us against war with Germany.

First, a reference to the plan embodied in our thirty treaties—the principle of which has been accepted by Germany. Her mention of arbitration opens the way and makes the suggestion easy, if it does not in fact compel the suggestion. It will ensure a peaceful settlement of this controversy. . . .

Second, steps to prevent passenger ships from carrying ammunition. This is referred to by Germany. Action ought, in my judgment, to be taken before the reply is sent.

Third, before we send another note to Germany, I think we should make a renewed protest to Great Britain against interference with our trade with neutrals. These three propositions have been under consideration before. The first was decided upon—that is the idea was given to the public and communicated to Germany—but you were dissuaded by something that you heard. The second is thought by the Attorney General to be possible—and even if it could not be accomplished as a matter of fact, the same end could be reached almost as well by advice such as was given to Americans in Mexico. The third suggestion was about to be carried out but you were dissuaded by a message from Mr. House."

Without doing these things, Bryan feared that the note Wilson outlined in cabinet meeting would be likely to cause a rupture of diplomatic relations which might rush us into a war in spite of anything we might do.

"If the initiative were with us I would not fear war, for I am sure you do not want it, but when the note is sent it is Germany's next move. . . . If the note causes her to act in an unfriendly way it may cause conditions here that will increase the difficulties of our position. This may be our last chance to speak for peace, for it will be much harder to propose investigation after some unfriendly act than *now*."[157]

That same day Wilson replied, and his letter meant that Bryan had been defeated:

"I hope that you realize how hard it goes with me to differ with you in judgment about such matters as we are now handling. You

[157] *Ibid.*, Bryan to Wilson, June 5, 1915.

always have such weight of reason, as well as such high motives, behind what you urge that it is with deep misgiving that I turn from what you press upon me. I am inclined to think that we ought to take steps, as you suggest, to prevent our citizens from travelling on ships carrying munitions of war, and I shall seek to find the legal way to do it. I fear that, whatever it may be best to do about that, it is clearly impossible to act before the new note goes to Germany.

"I am sorry to say that, study as I may the way to do it without hopelessly weakening our protest, I cannot find a way to embody in our note the principle of long discussion of a very simple statement of facts; and I think that our object with England can be gained better by not sending a note in connection with this one than by sending it; and, after all, it is our object and the relief of our trade that we want to accomplish.

"I recast the note last night. I hope you will think a little better of it.

"I would be very much obliged if you would go over it, for instance making any suggestions that may occur to you, and that you will ask Mr. Lansing to go over it for form and validity of statement and claim."[158]

It is significant that Bryan's influence led Wilson, at this point, to soften the terms of the note. In submitting to the President the re-draft made by Lansing, Bryan explained at great length his objections and his counter-suggestions. Wilson had used the *Gulflight* and *Cushing* incidents as justification for condemning the establishment of a war zone. It seemed to Bryan that in view of the fact that we accepted Germany's offer of apologies and reparations in the case of the attack of neutral vessels by mistake, that it was an unnecessary enlargement of our demand which really weakened the demand itself.

"Our interest in the war zone ceases to be acute if the right for which we ask is recognized—namely, that time will be allowed for passengers to escape. While there is force in the suggestion that they should avoid the zone, mistakes are liable to occur; still what we are really demanding of them is that everywhere, whether in any particular zone or upon the seas generally the belligerents shall not sink a merchantman without giving the crew and passengers time to escape."

[158] Wilson to Bryan, June 5, 1915, *Letter Book.*

Bryan also took issue with the sentence stating that there was no adequate compensation for the lives of the two seamen lost in the *Gulflight*. The sentence raised a question which was nowhere answered in the note. If there could be no adequate compensation for the loss of life of these two seamen, how were we to settle this particular case? Would it not be well to indicate the manner in which this claim could be adjusted? Did the President mean that, although a pecuniary compensation be accepted, it could not be adequate for the loss of life? This would indicate, that, in this particular case, damages would be accepted, "the vessel having been attacked without intention." If money was not to be accepted in such cases, then what compensation did the President have in mind? The punishment of the officer, or the physical punishment of the government responsible for it? It was unfortunate, Bryan observed, to raise an inquiry and then leave it a matter of doubt as to what would be acceptable, or to leave the impression that nothing whatever could be done to atone for the mistake.

Still another point in Wilson's draft troubled Bryan. The sentence referring to arguments made by Germany on the freedom of the seas seemed to be a surplusage calculated to offend.

"It detracts from the dignity of the paper to turn aside from the main discussion to answer an argument not involved in the controversy. In discussing the *Falaba* some attention should be paid to the assertion that failure to give sufficient time to the crew and passengers to escape was due to the alleged fact that "suspicious steamers" were hurrying to aid. This statement raises two questions, one of law and one of fact. If it is a fact (we have no other evidence) it can't be overlooked. The second point, if it were true, would it be justification for sinking the vessel?"

Bryan had asked Lansing to look for precedents—he would not feel like answering this question from intuition, and he could not answer it on information without knowing precedents. Did the effort of another vessel to rescue it have the same effect as a continued effort to escape? Or must the attacking vessel withdraw if it saw a vessel of superior force approaching before it was able to rescue passengers?

Bryan advised softening various phrases regarding the *Lusitania* in such a way as to make Germany's problem of backing water more easy. Indeed, in the whole discussion of the *Lusitania,* the note appeared to Bryan to speak as if our own statement of the facts foreclosed further discussion. He did not think either side had the right to assert a statement of facts, and then act upon the theory that there could be no further dispute. Would it not be proper to say that we had stated the facts as we believed them to exist, and that this statement, if true, would seem to remove the grounds upon which Germany based her departure from the rules governing prizes, and that if she was satisfied that these facts were erroneous, we should feel sure that she would be pleased to acknowledge that a grave mistake had been made? If she felt she had reason to question the facts as we had stated them, a joint investigation would be the proper way of arriving at the true facts.

He also suggested using in other places in the note words less calculated to offend, and particularly took issue on the point of omitting a paragraph written in the language of a friend which, it seemed clear, added strength to the note.

In concluding, Bryan pointed out that the note, as it stood, rendered it unnecessary for Great Britain to make any concessions. In fact, she would be encouraged not to do so. Would not Wilson announce that, pending negotiations with Germany on the use of the submarine, clearance would be refused to belligerent ships carrying American passengers and to American passenger ships carrying munitions?[159]

On Friday, June 4, after a confusing cabinet meeting, Bryan indicated to the President that he could not sign the note unless it was modified,[160] and that he thought it would be unfair for all concerned if he remained in the cabinet. When the finished note was sent that evening to the state department he knew a difficult decision must be made. He passed an almost sleepless night. If he resigned, he would be abused, vilified and misrepresented.[161]

[159] Bryan to Wilson, June 7, 1915.

[160] Houston, *Eight Years in Wilson's Cabinet,* I, 139; *Memoirs of William Jennings Bryan,* 422-423.

[161] *Memoirs,* 423.

But he was certain he must resign. If he waited until the note was sent, and a curt rejoinder returned, it would then be too late. If he should resign now, he might bring the real sentiments of the people, which he believed to be pacific, to the surface. These thoughts kept running through his mind: he could not sleep. The next day, Saturday, found him at his work as usual.[162] Then, about luncheon time, he went to McAdoo's house. His face was haggard; he was nervous. The Secretary of the Treasury had never seen him so agitated before. Bryan told him his decision to resign if the *Lusitania* note were sent, since he thought it would surely lead to war with Germany. His usefulness as secretary of state was over, he added. McAdoo replied that the note would not lead to war, and that he could not make a graver mistake than to resign. If he resigned, it would create the impression that there was a difference of opinion in the cabinet over a serious situation, and his act would contribute to the very result he was anxious to avoid.[163] Bryan sat silently and thoughtfully for a while. Then he said that he must abide by his own conscience: there was no alternative but to resign. That afternoon McAdoo went to the Bryan house, told Mrs. Bryan that her husband ought not to resign, and urged her to influence him to stay on. She remarked that he had been unhappy in his position for some time because of Wilson's habit of preparing important diplomatic papers himself. Her husband had come to feel that he was playing the part of a figurehead. McAdoo replied that he was sure the President had no thought of minimizing Mr. Bryan; that he submitted the notes, for which he was responsible, to the Secretary, and was glad to have his counsel and assistance. Then he proposed that the Bryans spend the week-end out of town, think matters over, and postpone a decision.[164] They agreed, and went to Senator Blair Lee's beautiful old home, Silver Spring. But the quiet of the country, the night song of the birds, the loveliness of the magnolia tree under which Bryan had spent many happy hours, brought no

[162] *Ibid.*
[163] William G. McAdoo, *Crowded Years,* 333.
[164] *Ibid.,* 333-334.

peace. He tossed and worried, trying to forget things by reading a book printed in 1829—"A Wreath of Appreciation of Andrew Jackson." The next morning he walked and talked with Senator Blair for hours. Only a powder brought sleep that night.[165]

Meantime McAdoo went to the White House and told the President of Bryan's intention of resigning. His father-in-law was not surprised. He knew the Secretary of State had been growing more and more out of sympathy in the controversy with Germany. He would like to have Bryan remain in the cabinet if it was possible. At this critical moment his resignation might lead Berlin to think there were wide differences within the administration. The President asked McAdoo to try to change Bryan's mind. But there was no use. He urged every consideration on him. Suppose he should be wrong, and the *Lusitania* note lead to a settlement of the issue rather than to war: how ridiculous Bryan would appear to the country. His career would be ruined. He would be condemned for having resigned in order to embarrass the administration. "I believe you are right," Bryan answered. "I think this will destroy me; but whether it does or not, I must do my duty according to my conscience, and if I am destroyed, it is, after all, merely the sacrifice that one must not hesitate to make to serve his God and his country."[166] With equally fruitless results Lansing also tried to dissuade Bryan.[167]

That same day—June 7—Bryan went to the White House. There was an earnest and calm interview, lasting an hour. Wilson refused to yield a point; Bryan would not, either. That night the resignation was sent and almost immediately accepted. "I accept your resignation," Wilson wrote him, "only because you insist upon its acceptance; and I accept it with much more than deep regret, with a feeling of personal sorrow. . . . Even now we are not separated in the object we seek but only in the method by which we seek it. . . . Our objects are the same and we ought to

[165] *Memoirs*, 424.
[166] McAdoo, *op. cit.*, 336; Houston, *Eight Years in Wilson's Cabinet*, I, 140.
[167] Robert Lansing, "The Dangers of Neutrality," *Sat. Even. Post.*, Apr. 18, 1931, 6.

pursue them together. I yield to your desire only because I must
and wish to bid you Godspeed in the parting."[168] There is little
doubt that the President was sincere; he had a genuine affection
for Bryan, as well as an admiration for him.[169]

The next day, June 8, the cabinet met. Bryan's resignation
had not yet been announced, though it was noticed he was absent.
The revised note was discussed, and the question raised whether
it was sufficiently firm. The President then announced the resignation of Bryan, and asked whether there would be any objection
to having him come in for the discussion. There was none, and
he came. But leaning back in his chair with half closed eyes, he
said little. After the meeting, as if loath to leave them, he asked
his former colleagues to have lunch with him. Lane, Daniels,
Burleson, Wilson, Garrison and Houston accepted. "I have had
to take the course I have chosen," Bryan told them. "The President has had one view. I have had a different one. I have had
to act as I have thought best. I cannot go along with him in this
note. I think it makes for war. I believe that I can do more on
the outside to prevent war than I can do on the inside. I think I
can help the President more on the outside." Lane told him, "You
are the most real Christian I know." Bryan broke down completely and wept.[170]

When the second *Lusitania* note was released, violent abuse
was heaped on Bryan for resigning rather than accepting it, inasmuch as it was milder than the first note which he had signed.
Houston suggested that he had not thought the first note dangerous, since it merely opened the discussion, while the second one
meant trouble if Germany would not accept our view.[171] Bryan
himself gave another reason. On June 12 he issued a statement to
the effect that the note had been materially revised following the
presentation of his resignation. He had seen the final draft of the

[168] *Memoirs,* 407-408; William C. Redfield, *With Congress and Cabinet*
(N. Y., 1924), 102; Houston, *op. cit.,* I, 140-1.
[169] Wilson to Bryan, June 9, 1915; Bryan to Daniels, Feb. 13, 1924,
Bryan Papers, 35.
[170] Houston, *op. cit.,* I, 146.
[171] *Ibid.*

note just before his resignation *took effect.* But *"he had no knowledge of this change at the time his resignation was tendered and accepted."* This clause very much softened the note:

"If the Imperial German Government should deem itself to be in possession of convincing evidence that the officials of the Government of the United States did not perform these duties with thoroughness, the Government of the United States sincerely hopes that it will submit that evidence for consideration."[172]

Although this clause left open the course Bryan had all along insisted on, further discussion, he did not ask permission to withdraw his resignation. It is true that House and Attorney General Gregory thought him mistaken in believing that the note had been modified after he had seen it. House has also said that the sentence to which Bryan referred was discussed at the last cabinet meeting when his resignation was offered, and at which he was present, and that the entire message had been handed to him to read.[173] But this does not at all contradict Bryan's testimony: his resignation had been tendered and accepted the day before. Although he did not again refer to the change which had been made during subsequent attacks—loyalty to the administration restrained him—he did cherish the conviction that his suggestion and the amendment he proposed converted the second *Lusitania* note from "an ultimatum to an argument."[174] Though this may have been too strong a statement, it is clear that his influence did substantially modify the original draft of the note.

His resignation brought a storm of disapproval from many of the most influential newspapers of the country. The New York *World* and Henry Watterson of the Louisville *Courrier-Journal* agreed that Bryan's resignation was "unspeakable treachery, not only to the President, but to the nation."[175] At the most critical moment in his country's history, the Dallas *News* exclaimed, he had brought "confusion and danger into our relations with Germany" by championing her cause against our own. A New Mexico

---

[172] *Memoirs*, 408-409.
[173] Seymour, *The Intimate Papers of Colonel House*, II, 6.
[174] Bryan to Daniels, Mar. 11, 1924, *Bryan Papers*, 35.
[175] McAdoo, *Crowded Years*, 336.

journal thought this was the first mistake he had ever made in his life![176] A veteran newspaper man observed in the New York *Evening Post* that the press of the country had never before been so unanimous in expressing condemnation of a public figure.[177] Some took him to task; others rejoiced to be rid of him; most, it was true, condemned.

Yet some newspapers, particularly in the South and West, upheld the former secretary of state. The Akron *Beacon Journal* believed that in time his wisdom would become clear. Although, it continued, he had often been wrong, he was, in this case, "so sane, so sound, and so right," that his act would do much to atone for errors of judgment in the past. For declining to be a figurehead any longer the Dallas *Democrat* had only words of praise, while the Chattanooga *Times* commended him for surrendering a great office rather than a principle. His resignation, the Pittsburgh *Leader* said, made him a greater figure than he had ever before been. Of course the German-American press was warm in its commendations.[178]

Indeed, no one close to Bryan questioned for a moment his high-mindedness. Members of his family felt he could do nothing else, and some of his colleagues did not blame him for refusing to be a party to a policy which he felt convinced would plunge the country into war. Lansing, who knew he was acting on principle "without apparent consideration of the effect upon his personal fortunes," later admitted that Bryan's expectations as to the consequences of the note of June 9 were, at the time, in a measure justifiable.[179]

Others, too, understood and appreciated his motives. Perhaps five thousand telegrams poured in, many from newspaper editors in small towns, and by far the greater number of these messages

[176] *Bryan Papers*, clippings, 36.
[177] New York Evening *Post*, June 25, 1915.
[178] *Bryan Papers, Correspondence and clippings*, 36.
[179] Robert Lansing, "The Difficulties of Neutrality," *loc. cit.*, 6-7. See also Josephus Daniels, *The Life of Woodrow Wilson* (Chicago and Philadelphia, 1924), 142-143.

supported him in his action.[180] Equally touching were some of the letters from the diplomatic corps in Washington who, without committing themselves to an expression of the wisdom of his action, deeply deplored its consequences in separating them from his association.[181] Senator O'Gorman and other public men deeply deplored the necessity for the resignation, but applauded his consistent adherence to his ideals.[182] Richard Bartholdt, a veteran Republican congressman and advocate of peace, expressed profound admiration for his courageous course "to vindicate a sacred principle" as well as his own convictions. He was certain that the nation's peace had been preserved only through Bryan's great personal sacrifice. It alone, he thought, checked the forces of belligerency which were gaining ascendancy at the White House.[183] Even Roosevelt, who bore him no love, wrote Lodge that "if it was right to pass all those treaties, it is right now, and not only right, but necessary, to grant Germany's request and have a Commission of Inquiry to last for one year." He went on to lament that, as a result of "infernal peace propaganda," with which he linked the Bryan treaties, their purpose had been, unfortunately achieved: so much time had been consumed that the people were cold and indifferent to the insult our national honor had suffered.[184]

Bryan had, in short, some reason to expect that, by going to the people, he could arouse a great latent pacific sentiment which, effectively expressed, would keep us out of the war. If he had failed in some of the tests of his pacifism during the high office he held, he had not faltered in the greatest test of all. If he had

[180] *Bryan Papers,* 36. This is merely an estimate.

[181] The letters from Spring-Rice, Chinda, and the ministers from Colombia, Bolivia, Cuba, Peru and Denmark were particularly cordial and sincere in the regrets they expressed at the resignation. *Bryan Papers,* 36.

[182] *Bryan Papers,* 36, *passim.* The letter of Gov. George Cornell of Oklahoma to Bryan, June 15, 1915 (*Bryan Papers,* 28) is typical of the letters of approval which came from many loyal political friends.

[183] Bartholdt to Bryan, Oct. 9, 1915, *Bryan Papers,* 28, *Correspondence 1913-1925.*

[184] *Selections from the Correspondence of Theodore Roosevelt and Henry Cabot Lodge,* (N. Y., 1925), II, 459.

been unable to persuade the President to accept his policy, he had refused to accept that of the President. Perhaps the people would sustain him in the last great battle for peace he was now to fight, though some pacifists could not help feeling that the one tie which could keep the country out of the war had been broken.[185]

[185] Dunn, *op. cit.,* II, 275.

IV

THE LAST FIGHT FOR PEACE

Convinced that he could crystallize sentiment for keeping the country out of Europe's war, Bryan went again to the people. He opened his campaign in New York on the evening of June 19, 1915, speaking to an audience made up largely of the representatives of labor. Five days later some seventy thousand people tried in vain to pack into Madison Square Garden to hear him again tell how to keep out of the war. In these two speeches, partly extemporaneous and partly written, he laid down the substance of his program.[1]

Let the people speak! That was his challenge. For surely they preferred reason to force, surely they had no desire to plunge into a maelstrom of blood and ruin. Let the people tell the President how they felt! True, this was no easy matter. It was so much easier for small minorities to pour into his ears what they would have him hear; and the metropolitan press, pretending to speak in the name of public opinion, sympathetically took on its shoulders half their load. It was a paying policy, Bryan assured his audience, for the newspapers to magnify international differences; and besides, they directly represented the munition makers and war traders—about that there was small doubt. No wonder then that the voice of the great, inert but peace-loving mass was drowned out by the clamor of special groups whose interest it was to promote the martial spirit.

To labor especially Bryan appealed for aid in the work of mobilizing public opinion for peace. No group suffered more from the burdens of war and its aftermath. It possessed an organization and machinery for propaganda. Would it help?[2]

---

[1] The following summary of these speeches is based on the manuscript drafts in the *Bryan Papers,* 28, and on accounts in the New York *Times,* June 20 and June 25, 1915.

[2] Gompers declared that labor was squarely behind Wilson, and that the meeting which Bryan addressed in no way represented American labor. Frank Buchanan, member of Congress from Illinois, had for some time

Bryan warned his listeners particularly against two movements which were already whipping into shape the public opinion which was so much at the mercy of the press. One minimized the effectiveness of our army and navy in order to furnish arguments for enlarging our military establishment. Roosevelt, discrediting as he did the motives and intelligence of peace men and agitating for an army and navy which would make us rival the great military Powers of the Old World, was the most important leader of this group. He would have us prepare against present dangers, overlooking the fact that the preparedness necessary to meet "present danger" would be inadequate for the future when other Powers augmented their armaments in response to our increase. Here Bryan sounded the note he was to repeat so often in the following months when preparedness came to be accepted by Wilson and an ever increasing number of powerful persons.

The other organization to be combated was led by Taft—it was the League to Enforce Peace which had been formed at Philadelphia only a few days before. While Roosevelt's defense societies aimed to make preparation for war pleasant, Taft's people furnished a plausible pretext for that preparation. It was nothing less than the use of force to fight force. It was indeed true that a forest fire was fought by fire. But Bryan reminded his listeners that fighting the devil with fire had never succeeded— he was so much better acquainted with it than his adversaries and at no expense for fuel! The plan of the League to Enforce Peace would render us partners with Europeans in waging war to make peace; we were to abandon Washington's advice about "entangling alliances." Why should we forget that our appeal had always been, not to the fears of the world, but to its heart and conscience? Akin to all the belligerents because of our heterogeneous population, why should we forfeit our great opportunity to act as a medi-

been trying to commit labor to pacifist propaganda, but had been unable to swing the A. F. L. at its meeting in Atlantic City. New York *Herald*, June 21, 1915. On June 22 representatives of a number of labor organizations met at Washington and laid plans for an aggressive peace campaign, but this meeting was also repudiated by Gompers. *Christian Herald*, July 7, 1915.

ator? Why should we abandon our example to the world of a
nation achieving beneficent ends by peace rather than by force?

But Bryan did not confine himself to generalities. He pointed
out, referring to violations of our neutral rights, that the grievances
we suffered did not result from the desire of the belligerents to
injure us: the trouble was that they were so angry fighting each
other that they forgot there was anyone else in the world. They
were like street brawlers unintentionally knocking down by-
standers. It was bad enough to go to war to avenge intended
wrongs: God forbid that we go to war to avenge those that were
unintended.[3]

The machinery for solving our problems lay at hand. Bryan
had not forgotten his treaties! Had he succeeded in signing a
treaty with Germany, not even the jingoes could have dragged us
into war. If the principle embodied in the treaties was good
enough to be offered to Germany, and good enough to be accepted
by her in principle, it was good enough to be used now or whenever
diplomatic methods failed. While the discussion and investigation
proceeded, we should expect Germany to avoid the creation of any
more embarrassment, and we on our part should prevent our
citizens from taking passage on ships of belligerents carrying
contraband.[4] It was indeed not a denial of justice to continue a
case because of the sickness of important witnesses—all Europe
was sick; it was not a denial of justice to take a change of *venue*
from a community where passion ran riot to one in which justice
could be administered calmly and impartially. This was the position
he had maintained in his late office.

In addition to the machinery of pause and delay, he made
another proposal—a somewhat more revolutionary one. It was
nothing less than government ownership and operation of munition
and armament plants. That would rid the country of the menace
of a sordid private interest which sailed under the false flag of
patriotism. A resolution to this effect was carried at the initial

[3] *Ibid.*
[4] Bryan was to inspire the introduction into Congress of resolutions
warning Americans against taking this unnecessary risk.

meeting to which Bryan made this appeal;[5] and other meetings followed suit.

These were the fundamental ideas which Bryan advanced for preventing war. As time went on, he developed and elaborated them; gave them new and striking applications when events turned one way or another; and reiterated them in dozens of speeches from one corner of the country to another. This was not, to be sure, his whole program. Remembering his conviction that loans from neutrals to belligerents made partisans of their creditors and gamblers on the outcome of the war, he denounced such loans whenever new ones were floated.[6] Holding fast to his faith in the virtue of the majority, he also advanced the idea, novel in the middle class peace movement, of a referendum on the question of peace and war. Although the Populists had made a good deal of the idea of popular referendum, they do not seem to have applied it to the question of war and peace. This proposal had indeed never been favored by the American peace movement. A Spanish senator and publicist had advanced it as early as 1870; German Socialists had sponsored it a little later; and LaFollette was to advocate it in 1916.[7] Bryan first proposed this plan in October, 1915,[8] and thereafter urged it as a safeguard and as an example to the nations of Europe.

[5] New York *Times,* June 20, 1915. As early as 1900 Claude Kitchin advocated building ships and armor plate in government plants. This plan was related to the anti-trust sentiment. *Cong. Record,* 56 cong. 1 sess., 33 Pt. V, Apr. 16, 1900, 4256 ff. Wilson also thought that the making and sale of arms and munitions should be a government monopoly. *Memoirs of William Jennings Bryan,* 391.

[6] New York *Times,* Sept. 17, Sept. 29, 1915.

[7] Senor Don A. du Marcoartu in the *Sessional Proceedings of the National Association for the Promotion of Social Science for the year 1870-1871,* 206; Theodore D. Woolsey, *Communism and Socialism in their History and Theory* (London, 1879), 118-19, 232. Robert Beasley (*A Plan to Stop the Present and Prevent Future Wars,* (Rio Vista, California, 1863), proposed a popular referendum, with compulsory voting, on continuing or immediately concluding the Civil War.

[8] New York *Times,* Oct. 18, 1915. The *Times* editorially denounced Bryan for the proposal. "Mr. Bryan's mind is the Happy Valley, the Fortunate Isles. It is a wonderful possession, unique among the treasures of the world." Oct. 19, 1915.

Before analysing this program and Bryan's strategy in trying to realize it, we note that it did not include an embargo on arms and munitions. We have seen that Bryan had opposed such a measure while still secretary of state,[9] and he now continued to resist the pressure which German-American groups put on him to embrace the embargo plan. Indeed, it had been advocated at the two meetings in New York at which Bryan inaugurated his crusade against our entering the war. One of them incorporated the embargo idea in its resolutions. After that Bryan insisted on expressing his own opposition to an embargo on arms if such a proposition were to be included in resolutions at meetings which he addressed. He believed that there was no possibility of enacting an embargo act and that its advocacy destroyed the influence of the organizations urging such an act. Besides, he was convinced that an embargo would clearly violate our neutrality since it would so obviously help Germany; the press therefore would find an excuse to discredit the whole peace movement unless the embargo program were dropped. "My sole interest," he wrote to Henry Weismann, president of the United German Societies of New York, "is in keeping this country out of war with *any* belligerent and I am just as much afraid of helping one side as I am of helping the other."[10] The Neutrality League of St. Louis refused to pay the five hundred dollars he asked for speaking on peace unless he would favor an embargo; but he was not tempted.[11] When the "Friends of Peace" held a convention in Chicago on September 7, 1915, he participated only on condition that no resolution on an embargo be offered.[12] The New York *American* took the Nebraskan to task for his position. How could he be considered a consistent or wholly sincere friend of peace, it asked, when he advocated the

[9] Letter of Bryan to Senator Stone, Jan. 20, 1915, in New York *Times,* Jan. 25, 1915.
[10] Bryan to Weismann, Aug. 27, 1915, and Bryan to Mr. Walker, Aug. 28, 1915. *Bryan Papers,* 36.
[11] New York *Times,* July 9, 1915.
[12] *Ibid.,* Sept. 5, 1915, Sept. 7, 1915. Bryan's rival in the Democracy of Nebraska, Senator Gilbert Hitchcock, did coöperate with the Embargo Conference, organized in Chicago in 1915. George Sylvester Viereck, *Spreading Germs of Hate,* (N. Y., 1930), 99.

sale and exportation of arms to nations using them to make war
and murder each other's people? If Bryan were in favor of the
sale of liquor and were running a bar could he be considered a
sincere and consistent advocate of temperance?[13]

Such was Bryan's plan for keeping us out of the war. In many
respects his analysis of the dangers involved in the situation and
his concrete proposals were realistic and intrinsically admirable.
It should have appealed to the common man, the plain people. It
was not mere shallow sentimentalism. On the contrary, the heir
of the Populists clearly understood some of the economic causes
of war, and suggested remedies which should still command the
respect of those believing that the causes of war are largely economic and psychological. Propaganda, inspired by desire for
profit; loans to belligerents, committing us to their cause; an
armament trust identifying patriotism with thirst for gold; priv-
ileged Americans insisting on travelling to Europe in *de luxe* cabins
of belligerent vessels at the risk of endangering the lives of hundreds of thousands of humbler citizens in war; all these things
were both relevant and fundamental. If his preventive measures
seem less realistic, still they were worthy of trial. Who can say
that investigation, delay, and patience might not have been effective? Taken all in all, Bryan's program was comprehensive and
plausible. Viewed from the standpoint of his contemporaries, it
might well have proved effective. Why did he fail to carry the
people with him?

A possible reason is that Bryan was regarded as a false prophet.
Had he not been wrong in 1896? Had he not been wrong in the
Lusitania matter? The stiff note brought no war, though he had
predicted it would. What seemed to be a successful outcome of
Wilson's policy robbed Bryan of much of his thunder. It was
perhaps for that reason that he did not devote all his energy to
his fight. The chautauqua claimed a share of his time; and a great
deal of his enthusiasm went into the cause of prohibition and the

[13] New York *American*, June 26, 1915.

campaign for woman suffrage.[14] Who can say whether he might not have accomplished more had he scattered his energies less?

Probably a much greater obstacle to the advance of his peace program, however, was the attitude of the influential newspapers. The cause of peace was not popular in the press, which in general was committed to the promotion of the interests of advertisers who saw good business in preparedness and Allied success. Often it was necessary to pay for notices of peace meetings, and these notices generally appeared in obscure places in the newspapers.[15] More significant, however, was the fact that the leading journals insisted that Bryan was playing politics. The New York *World* excoriated him for pretending to support Wilson when it was obvious that he was coveting the President's leadership. It denounced his course as a partisan and rancorous crusade.[16] No less biting was the New York *Times* which again and again gave editorial space to bitter denunciations and to plain declarations that this entire peace campaign was motivated by jealousy of his former chief and by presidential aspirations.[17] After Bryan's support of the President in the campaign of 1916, the *Times* tried to make every peace action it reported appear treasonable or ridiculous. It now spared no pains to fight the peace crusader. Although Bryan talked to dozens of organizations for no fee at all, the *Times* gave great publicity to his refusal to speak in St. Louis before the Neutrality League unless it could guarantee an attendance of 50,000 and an honorarium of five hundred dollars.[18] He was made to seem a grasping, mercenary man who demanded his gold even for a cause to which he appeared so devoted.

Worse even than these attacks was the persistent effort to play up the fact that Bryan had begun his peace campaign by speaking to a group largely German-American in its makeup. At his second

[14] *Memoirs of William Jennings Bryan*, 432-433; Dunn, *From Harrison to Harding*, II, 296-297.

[15] *Memoirs*, 436.

[16] New York *World*, June 26, 1915.

[17] New York *Times*, June 22, 26, 1915; Nov. 7, 1915, Dec. 10, 1915; Mar. 7, 1916.

[18] *Ibid.*, July 3, 9, 28, 1915.

New York meeting he had been introduced by Henry Weismann, a prominent German-American, and the Austrian and German embassies were well represented.[19]   The Washington *Herald* observed that he could have made no converts among his audience since he merely put their views into his own words,[20] while the New York *Sun*—taunted him with a cheap jibe—"O Bottom, Bottom, how art thou translated into Boy-Orator-of-the-Platte-Deutsch!"[21]   The Philadelphia *Record*[22] likewise emphasized the pro-German character of this meeting and wondered why it had not been held in Berlin.   More seriously, the New York *World*, heading its editorial with the words "When Sedition is Afoot,"[23] made the most of the "pro-German" character of some of the resolutions adopted at the Madison Square demonstration.   The New York *Times* called attention to the pleas in the *Staats-Zeitung* for a full German attendance, and the "royal response" to these pleas.[24]   It would be easy to cite a dozen such attacks.   Although they were quite unjustified, there was enough basis for them to convince Bryan that it had been a tactical mistake to speak at a meeting in which German-Americans played so large a part.   But greater caution did not repair the damage already done.   Nor did the proposal of his name for the Nobel peace prize by a member of the Austrian parliament help matters.[25]

Equally unfortunate was the publicity given to Bryan's plans for going to Europe to help end the war, plans which were made to appear more ridiculous, more egotistical and more melodramatic than was the actual case.   As early as February, 1914, he had thought of giving peace lectures in Europe's leading capitals,[26] but Page's frantic remonstrances apparently had their effect. The Secretary of State had also considered a personal visit to London and Berlin for trying to end the war, and must have been disappointed

[19] *Ibid.*, July 3, 9, 19, 1915.
[20] Washington *Herald*, June 26, 1915.
[21] New York *Sun*, June 26, 1915.
[22] Philadelphia *Record*, June 26, 1915.
[23] New York *World*, June 26, 1915.
[24] New York *Times*, June 26, 1915.
[25] *Ibid.*, Mar. 16, 1916.
[26] Burton J. Hendrick, *Life and Letters of Walter Hines Page*, I, 235.

when Colonel House announced that he had been chosen for such a mission.[27] After his resignation, Bryan very seriously thought of carrying out his long-considered purpose. Individuals and organizations encouraged him. Richard Bartholdt, a former member of Congress and founder of the American group of the Interparliamentary Union, urged him to go, pointing out that almost certainly something might be accomplished if European neutrals could be assured that any initiative they took for negotiations between the belligerents would be regarded sympathetically by the United States. "I cannot see how the President can decline to give his blessing to such an undertaking," continued Bartholdt, "for even if the slaughter, as a result of it, were shortened only one day, the attempt would yet be worth while. If the President is unwilling, as he seems to be, to take the initiative himself, he cannot well object to others taking it."[28] Authorities in the Federal Council of Churches of Christ in America joined with foreign language newspapers in likewise urging him to try his hand at peacemaking in Europe.[29] On August 13, 1915, House wrote to Page that Bryan had apparently decided on such a course. Knowing that the former secretary of state stood high in the estimation of Berlin, House feared that he would strengthen the impression that American pacifism was so strong that Germany might with impunity pursue an uncompromising course. But Page no longer dreaded the coming of his former chief—he would cut "no more figure than a tar-baby at a negro camp-meeting" he wrote assuringly to the Colonel; and the latter concluded that he would probably come back "a sadder and wiser man."[30] Bryan's plans for going to Europe became public property, and the vindictive New York *Times* poked no end of fun at his "heroic resolve" and

[27] Charles Seymour, *The Intimate Papers of Colonel House*, I, 352.

[28] Bartholdt to Bryan, Oct. 9, 1915, *Bryan Papers*, 28.

[29] Shailer Mathews to Bryan, Oct. 11, 1915, *ibid.*; minutes taken in an informal meeting of some New York editors of foreign language journals, *ibid.*; F. L. Seely to Bryan, Aug. 3, 1915, *Bryan Papers*, 36; New York *Times*, Sept. 18, 19, 23, 1915.

[30] Charles Seymour, *The Intimate Papers of Colonel House*, II, 18, 19, 21; Burton J. Hendrick, *The Life and Letters of Walter Hines Page*, II 12-13.

"sublime endeavor." When it looked as if after all he would stay at home to fight preparedness, the *Times* insinuated that there could be no reason for such a decision other than a pecuniary one— he did not want to forfeit his fat fees for spreading his Master's gospel of peace. What a pity, it added, since his exportation at his own expense would be a blessing: the silver-tongued orator could "hardly do this country more harm abroad than he has done it at home."[31]

These scathing remarks were nothing in comparison with the ridicule heaped on Bryan for his part in the Ford peace ship fiasco. As early as September 15, 1915, he was in Detroit consulting with the auto magnate[32] and of course was invited to join the peace ship crusade. On November 26, 1915, the New York *Times* announced that Ford had asked him to be first mate.[33] Secretary of the Navy Daniels favored his acceptance; Cave Johnson thought it a move- ment from which good might come; the owner of the Cologne *Gazette* urged him to participate by holding out the inducement that both the German government and people were favorable to the move; and it was reported that even President Wilson's heart went out to Ford's earnest and simple appeals for support.[34] Bryan finally decided, however, not to sail with the peace ark, though he smilingly blessed the pacifists as the *Oscar II* steamed away from its New York dock.[35] Possibly the unfavorable news- paper publicity, with which he had been associated, played some part in his decision. When a reporter asked Mr. Ford's publicity agent whether Bryan were going, he is said to have replied, 'Not if we can help it'—and this insolent remark was played up in every sheet.[36] The Great Commoner decided to be cautious, to wait until he could see how the peace crusade made out. Only when news came that Ford had abandoned his colleagues at Christiania did Bryan cancel his passage for The Hague—at which place he

---

[31] New York *Times,* Sept. 19, 21, 1915.
[32] New York *Times,* Sept. 15, 1915.
[33] *Ibid.,* Nov. 26, 1915.
[34] Seely to Bryan, Asheville, N. C., Dec. 7, 1915, *Bryan Papers,* 28.
[35] New York *Times,* Dec. 4, 1915.
[36] Louis P. Lochner, *America's Don Quixote,* (London, 1924), 28-39.

had half promised to meet the crusaders.[37] But his connection
with the affair had been sufficient to deepen the impression on the
part of a great many people that this was the sort of ridiculous
vagary that might be expected from the great pacifist.[38] As a
matter of fact, Bryan still cherished the hope that he might go to
Europe to plead for peace. In December, 1916, he told the Rev.
Charles S. Macfarland that the failure of the Federal Council of
Churches to dispatch him as a peace emissary was the deepest disappointment in his life—and he was almost if not actually in tears.

But it was not only his connection with the Ford affair that
brought ridicule from an influential portion of the press. While
many of his arguments against preparedness were telling, he occasionally made statements which, taken out of their context, appeared so naïve as to be ridiculous. "The President knows that
if this country needed a million men, and needed them in a day,"
he had said in December, 1914, "the call would go out at sunrise
and the sun would go down on a million men in arms." What
Bryan meant, of course, was that in case of actual invasion Americans would rise up *en masse* to defend their homes. But the New
York *Times* editorially asserted that no more foolish words had
ever been spoken by mortal man.[39] It was easy to point out that
the task involved in equipping such an army would be an arduous
one, and that Bryan was more lyrical than logical. Similar derision
was called out when in his antipreparedness campaign during the
autumn of 1915, he advocated, as the best possible type of defence,
the construction of twelve great national roads useful in time of
peace and serviceable in time of emergency for mobilizing a
citizen-soldiery.[40] These ideas were given undue emphasis in the

[37] New York *Times,* Dec. 1, and Dec. 28, 1915.
[38] Bryan was asked to be a correspondent of the Conference for Con-
tinuous Mediation, which grew out of the Ford Peace Ship crusade, and
apparently consented. Emily Greene Balch, Sept. 7, 1916 to Bryan, *Bryan
Papers, Miscel. Letters 1900-1922.* The Conference gave wide publicity in
Europe to Bryan's letter of Nov. 10, 1916, to Bucher Heller, President of
the Swiss Peace Society, on the necessity of the belligerents' stating their
terms. *Misc. Letters,* Louis Lochner to Bryan, (no date).
[39] New York *Times,* Dec. 11, 1914.
[40] *Ibid.,* Sept. 9, 1915.

press which neglected to feature many of the wise and sensible arguments which he was making. These words it ignored:

"The question is not whether a nation will resist an attack if an attack is actually made. Of course, no one thinks that is the question at issue in the United States today. The real question is whether, under the guise of preparing for defence, we shall load ourselves down with unnecessary taxes, stir up a war spirit in the country, create a military class among us, adopt false standards of honor, swagger about and by threats excite hatreds which lead to war. The advocates of peace believe that the philosophy which preserves peace in a neighborhood is the best assurance of international peace, and they seek to substitute the spirit of peace, which acts through friendship, for the spirit of war, which acts through ultimatum."[41]

He was even less fortunate in his attacks on the Navy League and the National Security League. Convinced that private interests again and again influenced public action by covering selfishness with a patriotic mask, Bryan not unnaturally inferred that organizations favoring preparedness derived support from shipbuilders and munition-makers. In a speech in Philadelphia on November 3, 1915, he was reported as having made such a charge.[42] At once the patriotic organizations thus attacked were on their heels. Both offered to have their books audited to prove that they had never taken a penny from either munition-makers or shipbuilders, and the Navy League went so far as to threaten suit unless Bryan proved his statement or made a public denial.[43] He could only say that he had been misquoted.[44] Some might believe that there was none the less substantial truth in the indictment credited to him; but the majority who read this stir in the newspapers probably concluded that it was one more evidence of his untrustworthiness.

[41] "The War in Europe and its Lesson for US," *Advocate of Peace* LXXVII, no. 11, Dec. 1915, 257 ff. The New York *Times,* Nov. 30, 1915, made a brief reference to this article, which resembles many speeches Bryan had been making.
[42] New York *Times,* Nov. 5, 1915.
[43] *Ibid.,* Nov. 6, 11, 12, 24, 1915.
[44] *Ibid.,* Nov. 12.

In his efforts to commit the Democratic party to antipreparedness Bryan had to encounter the great influence of the President.
In his address before the Manhattan Club,[45] he had openly sponsored preparedness—perhaps because he feared that on this issue
Roosevelt was winning the people over to the Republican camp.
The veteran leader of the Democracy could not believe that the
party which had opposed tariffs, trusts and imperialism could be
brought to sponsor a policy which meant an increase of taxation,
promotion of jingoism, and commitment to false standards of patriotism—a return, in short, to the swagger of the pistol-toter and
the sham honor of the duelist.[46] He could not believe that the great
body of the people would sanction a false philosophy which had
obviously brought Europe to disaster, which Latin-America would
feel bound to copy, and which meant a complete abandonment of
our national policy and a repudiation of Christian principles.[47]
Claude Kitchin, member of the House Committee on appropri-
ations, sharing his views, half promised support,[48] and there was
still a small but loyal squad of congressmen who swore by Bryan.[49]
Nevertheless the gossips of Washington were not altogether wrong
in guessing that the Great Commoner's break with Wilson on preparedness meant political death.[50] One after another the influential newspapers of the South took their stand against him.[51] Early
in January the fifth Mississippi district elected an anti-Bryan man
who had made preparedness the cornerstone of his campaign.[52]
In February Bryan took the stump, following closely on Wilson's

[45] "Outline of the Administration's Program of Preparedness for National Defense," Nov. 4, 1915, *The New Democracy*, I, 384-392.
[46] New York *Times*, Oct. 16, Nov. 6, Nov. 7, 1915.
[47] *Ibid.*
[48] Claude Kitchin to Bryan, Sept. 10, 1915, *Bryan Papers*, 36. Kitchin
later, however, disclaimed any purpose of balking the President. New York
Times, Nov. 15, 1915.
[49] Bryan's most ardent supporters in the House were W. W. Bailey of
Pennsylvania, Slayden and Dies of Texas, Tavenner of Illinois, Sanders of
Virginia, and Hensley of Missouri.
[50] New York *Times*, Nov. 5, 1915.
[51] For comments of the Birmingham *News*, Houston *Chronicle*, Mont-
gomery *Advertiser*, Austin *American*, Charleston *News and Courier*, Dallas
News, and the Arkansas *Gazette* see New York *Times*, Nov. 15, 1915.
[52] New York *Times*, editorial, Jan. 12, 1916.

heels as he invaded the Middle West pleading for preparedness.[53]
The Peerless Leader argued:

"The President's preparedness program is revolutionary; it is an
abandonment of the historic policy of the party and the tendencies
of the country. He has departed from the safe path of experience
and is following the devious ways pointed out by the big papers
which voice the wishes of the manufacturers of munitions. He
is joy-riding with the jingoes and is applauded by grandstanders
whose voices are unfamiliar to Democratic ears."[54]

Neither his arguments nor his persuasive voice carried conviction. Even Nebraska turned against him: in the spring primaries
he stood sixth among the candidates for delegate-at-large to the
national convention.[55] True, the convention called him from the
press gallery to speak, and—he spoke for Wilson.[56] He might
have seized this dramatic opportunity to speak against preparedness. But in the test, he was too good a party man to occasion
cleavage on the eve of a presidential campaign. All summer he
urged the country to support Wilson because he had "kept us out
of war." In only one state in which Bryan campaigned did the
people by voting for Hughes fail to heed his advice. The election
was won, thanks in part to his persuasive appeals. But the campaign against preparedness had indeed already been lost. Though
he continued to oppose compulsory military service,[57] a train of

[53] *Ibid.*, Jan. 20, 25, Feb. 1, 1916.
[54] Editorial in *The Commoner*, cited in New York *Times*, Feb. 19, 1916.
[55] New York *Times*, Apr. 21, 1916.
[56] *Memoirs of William Jennings Bryan*, 440-441; New York *Times*, June 16, 1916.
[57] Percy E. Quinn (Miss.) to Bryan, Dec. 30, 1916, *Bryan Papers, Misc. Letters, 1900-1922*. Bryan thought that if such an "outrage" as compulsory military service were committed, the people would drive the party which was responsible out of power. At a meeting of educators when he de-nounced compulsory drill, he was enthusiastically applauded. New York *Times*, July 5, 1916. Other circumstances convinced Bryan of the opposition of the people to militarism. Thus, for example, Washington Gladden, in congratulating him on his part in the presidential campaign, expressed the belief that if Wilson had followed Bryan's lead, he would have carried forty-eight instead of thirty states. Gladden to Bryan, Nov. 20, 1916, *Bryan Papers*, 35. Bryan continued to urge his supporters in Congress to oppose compulsory military service until our entrance into the war. Bryan to Representatives W. W. Bailey, McKellar and Quinn, Dec. 23, 1916. *Bryan-Bailey Correspondence.*

quick, dramatic events disheartened him in the fight he continued to wage against our entering the war.

In the spring of 1916 he sponsored the introduction of resolutions in Congress to warn Americans against taking passage in ships of belligerents or those of neutrals carrying contraband. Senator Gore, who championed such a measure, admitted that he had taken counsel with Bryan on the subject; and in the House, 142 out of 418 voting congressmen favored the parallel McLemore resolution even after it had been denounced by Wilson.[58] The New York *Times* insisted that Bryan had inspired this "pro-German insurrection" and, denouncing him as "The Smiler with the Knife" it proclaimed that "the explosion in Congress is in great part the effect of his mines."[59] There can be no doubt that he used his influence to further the Gore and McLemore resolutions, and that he regarded the failure of the latter as no true test of the opinion of Congress on this issue.[60]

Defeated on this front, he became desperate. When events in April, 1916, threatened war with Germany, Bryan hurried on to Washington to try to prevent such an outcome. "I believe," he announced, that "it would be a crime against civilization to do anything that would increase the chances of going into the War."[61] With congressmen he argued that postponement would in all probability enable us to reach a settlement after the war; if it did not do that, at least a war would then be *our* war, and not that of Europe.[62] Sarcastically the New York *Times,* calling attention to the fact that he had just been defeated in the Nebraska primaries, remarked, "Doubtless Mr. Bryan has a few friends left. They should take him home."[63] Indeed, his political capital was low, and after thirty hours in Washington he himself realized his helplessness, and left. His metropolitan enemy at last admitted that he

[58] New York *Times,* Feb. 26, 1916, March 8, 1916; *Cong. Record,* 53, Pt. IV. Feb. 17, Feb. 22, Mar. 7 and Mar. 10, 1916, especially 3688 ff., 3720.

[59] New York *Times,* Feb. 26, 1916.

[60] *Ibid.,* Mar. 8, 1916.

[61] *Ibid.,* April 20.

[62] *Ibid.*

[63] *Ibid.,* Apr. 21, 1916.

had lost his power for mischief. "The capital was cold to him," it observed. "Nobody cared a rap about his views. He came. He failed. He went."[64]

But there was still hope. When Congress convened in December, 1916, Bryan was on hand, and his enthusiastic reception in the House of Representatives indicated that he still had some rope with which to work.[65] He took part in conferences which were being held by the friends of peace and worked as best he could to dampen the war spirit. Henry D. Flood, who favored our entrance into the struggle, quietly took a canvass among his colleagues in the lower house and found that, in the early days of the session, a majority opposed a declaration of war.[66] Best of all, Germany on December 12 made her overture for peace negotiations. Equally auspicious was the fact that the President seemed at last to have responded to the pleas Bryan had been making again and again during the last year: on December 18 Wilson sent his note to the belligerents asking them to state their aims and terms. No one could have congratulated Wilson more warmly than his former secretary of state.[67]

But he did more. Perhaps there was a chance for him personally to further the cause so close to his heart. Might not England be urged to enter into peace negotiations with Germany? Might not Germany be induced to state terms which would be so moderate that discussions must inevitably follow? Who could tell?

At any rate Bryan meant to try. Bernstorff, the German am-

[64] *Ibid.*, Apr. 23. Representative Isaac Sherwood, a Civil War veteran pacifist from Ohio, introduced a resolution proposing the application of the machinery of Bryan's treaty plan. New York *Times,* Apr. 29, 1916.

[65] Dunn, *From Harrison to Harding,* II, 348.

[66] Robert Lansing, "The Difficulties of Neutrality," *Sat. Evening Post,* Apr. 18, 1931, 104. As late as Feb. 9, 1917, Congressman W. W. Bailey of Johnstown, Penn., noted a lack of war sentiment among his constituents, and among others in various parts of the country from whom he heard. Bailey to Bryan, Feb. 9, 1917, *Bryan-Bailey Correspondence.*

[67] Bryan to Wilson (no date) *Bryan Papers,* 36; New York *Times,* Dec. 21, 1916. Bryan had urged the President to ask the belligerents to state their aims and terms on May 23 and on Dec. 5, 1915. Senator Hitchcock carried out Bryan's idea of a resolution requesting the President to ask the belligerents to state their terms. Henry F. Hollis to Bryan, Jan. 16, 1917, *Misc. Letters, 1914-1923.*

bassador at Washington, encouraged him by saying that he was
convinced the German peace terms would be "extremely reasonable," and that, moreover, the Allies must accept the suggestion to
discuss peace at The Hague unless they were willing to shoulder
the entire responsibility for continuing the war.[68] From the American ambassador in Berlin Bryan learned that the President's peace
note had been enthusiastically received by the Government and by
all but a conservative minority of the people.[69] Bryan was also in
touch with the Reverend Charles S. Macfarland, general secretary
of the Federal Council of Churches of Christ, who on December
20th informed him that he had resumed his wireless communica-
tions with the German chancellor and had made suggestions which,
he thought, would render it possible for the Allies to open negotiations. It was hoped that the German government might by quiet
pressure be persuaded to make to the Allies a reply free from
aggravating statements relative to German victories and ref-
erences to the causes of the war. Would not Bryan also urge the
Germans to frame a self-respecting but conciliatory reply committing them to disarmament and a world court as an earnest of
their pacific intentions?[70] Had Bryan acted on this suggestion he
would probably have been open to the charge of violating the
Logan act, a federal statute forbidding any private citizen to negotiate with a foreign Power unless by the authority of his own
government. He contented himself with expressing to the German
ambassador the hope that his government would state specific terms
—terms so reasonable as to lead to negotiations.[71]

Bryan also personally urged Lloyd George, the British premier,
to consider favorably the German peace overture of December 12.
On December 14 he sent a cable reminding him that the responsibility for continuing the war was even greater than that of starting it,
inasmuch as the war had proved far more horrible than anyone

[68] Bernstorff to Bryan, Dec. 18, Dec. 28, 1916, *Bryan Papers,* 34.
[69] Gerard to Bryan, Dec. 27, 1916, *Bryan Papers,* 34.
[70] Charles S. Macfarland, New York, Dec. 20, 1916, *Bryan Papers.*
[71] Bryan to the Rev. Charles Macfarland, Miami, Fla., Dec. 24, 1916, *ibid.*

could have imagined. The great pacifist begged the Welch war leader to secure his government's consent to peace negotiations:

"There is no dispute that must necessarily be settled by force. All international disputes are capable of adjustment by peaceful means. Every guarantee that can possibly be secured by war can be stated as a condition precedent to peace. Do not, I pray you, by refusing an exchange of views assume the responsibility for a continuation of the unspeakable horrors of this unparalleled conflict. Your decision may mean life or death to millions."[72]

Secretary of the Navy Daniels, in writing to Bryan, characterized this as a "strong appeal" and hoped that the Premier would think twice before rejecting a conference. It was not to be expected, he continued, that any belligerent would name its real and final terms at the start, but if a conference could be called, there was every reason to hope that a basis could be reached by which the awful slaughter might be ended.[73] Claude Kitchin, majority leader in the House, regarded the propositions in the message as "absolutely sound and irrefutable," and rejoiced that it had been sent.[74] Sir Cecil Spring-Rice, the British ambassador, thought that the cable would pass the censor,[75] but, like officials at the state department, held out little hope that the Allies would consider peace negotiations.[76] This was also the impression of John Barrett, director of the Pan-American Union, who had found, in his recent experiences in Europe, an overwhelming sentiment against any peace which did not comprehend a complete submission to German and Austrian aspirations on the one hand, or to those of England and France on the other.[77] Although Bryan was promised that his "clear and concise" message would reach ten million people through the Newspaper Enterprise Association,[78] it re-

[72] *Bryan Papers,* 36.
[73] Daniels to Bryan, Dec. 17, 1916, *Bryan Papers,* 35.
[74] Kitchin to Bryan, Dec. 19, 1916, *Bryan Papers, Misc. Letters, 1900-1922.*
[75] Sir Cecil Spring-Rice to Bryan, Dec. 17, 1917, *Bryan Papers,* 36.
[76] Benjamin G. Davis to Bryan, Jan. 1, 1917. Lansing feared that if Bryan's cable were sent through the embassy, it might be embarrassing.
[77] John Barrett to Bryan, Dec. 17, 1916, *Bryan Papers,* 23.
[78] Charles Stelzle to Bryan, Dec. 26, 1916, *Misc. Letters 1900-1922.*

ceived scant notice in the Washington and New York press.[79]   If
Lloyd George responded to Bryan's cable, there is no record of it
in the latter's papers.[80]   One more defeat!   His futile efforts to
assemble the belligerents, all of whom claimed to be fighting for the
same principles, and to insist that they live up to their professions
of peace, showed how dark the outlook was for an early end of the
war.   Wilson found that out when, on December 18, just three
days after Bryan's overture to Lloyd George appeared in the press,
he sent his identical note to the belligerent Powers.   He was himself acting in the same spirit that had prompted Bryan to send his
plea to Lloyd George, assuming, as he did, that there was no dispute which must be settled on the battlefield.   But his effort, so far
as ending the war went, was as barren as that of Bryan.[81]

Courageously Bryan again turned to the people.   In his address
sponsored by the American Neutral Conference Committee in
Madison Square Garden, February 2, 1917, he declared that every
question, save actual invasion alone, should be submitted to arbitration or investigation.   If this seemed impossible, then its settlement should be postponed until the end of the war.   To enter this
struggle, which was in no sense our own, would be to step down
from our high position as the greatest neutral Power and forfeit
the honor of bringing the war to a close.   The meeting enthusiastically adopted resolutions urging the President to call a conference
of neutrals for that purpose.[82]   Two days later the announcement
of the new submarine policy of Germany bewildered and embittered
American opinion.   Bryan appealed immediately to the people,

[79] Daniel V. Stephens, Dec. 20, 1916, to Bryan, *Misc. Letters 1900-1922;*
New York *Times,* Dec. 16, 1915.   Bailey, writing to Bryan, Dec. 21, 1916,
noted that the associated press carried Bryan's message, but that it was so
obscured as to be almost suppressed.   *Bryan-Bailey Correspondence.*

[80] In 1923 Lloyd George conveyed through Charles Dawes an affectionate
greeting and personal regard for Bryan's "character and ability."   Dawes to
Bryan, Oct. 18, 1923, *Bryan Papers,* 19.

[81] W. W. Bailey to Bryan, Washington, Dec. 21, 1916; and Jan. 5, 1917.
On Dec. 22 a resolution embodying the ideas of Wilson's note was introduced
into the House of Representatives.

[82] *Bryan Papers,* 29; New York *Times,* Feb. 3, 1917; W. W. Bailey to
W. Wilson, Feb. 3, 1917.   Seven thousand heard the address, which was one
of Bryan's best efforts.

urging them to let the President know their opposition to entering the war, and to press home on their representatives the fact that there were still several alternatives to war: postponement of outstanding issues until the European struggle was over; keeping Americans off belligerent ships; refusing clearance papers to American vessels carrying both contraband and passengers; and, if necessary, forbidding all American ships from entering the war zone. Only by a referendum ought the last, desperate step be taken.[83] This plea, which the press of the country quite generally noticed, was repeated at a meeting of the Anti-war League in Washington a few days later. Could the people be consulted, he insisted, nine-tenths would declare that we should defend ourselves against invasion, but that we should refuse to send to Europe a single American soldier to die in a cause which was not our own.[84] To governors with whom he had influence he begged for aid in opposing the demand for war.[85] Most of the replies were discouraging, though sometimes he was assured that the masses were standing by him.[86] True, hundreds of telegrams were received in Congress following his appeal to the country, and their resemblance to his own position convinced the New York *Times* that he had inspired them.[87] Several motions were offered in Congress demanding a referendum, and though there seemed to be some little sentiment in their favor, even their supporters scarcely hoped for a favorable report.[88] After all, no machinery existed for such a referendum, and constitutional amendments were painfully slow to make.[89]

When, late in February, it was understood that the President meant to ask Congress to confer on him undefined powers of action,

[83] New York *Times,* Feb. 4, 1917.
[84] *Ibid.,* Feb. 5, 1917.
[85] Gov. R. L. Williams to Bryan, Feb. 5, 1917, *Misc. Letters 1900-1922;* Gov. James M. Cox to Bryan, Feb. 5, 1917, *Bryan Papers,* 34.
[86] F. O. Lawson and John Wright, Greensboro, N. C., Feb. 6, 1917, to Bryan, *Misc. Letters 1900-1922;* Joseph Mesmer, Los Angeles, Feb. 22, 1917, *Misc. Letters 1914-1923.*
[87] New York *Times,* Feb. 7, 1917; *Cong. Rec.* 54, Part 3, 2662-2663. (64 Cong. 2d sess.).
[88] George Huddleson to Bryan, Feb. 13, 1917, *Misc. Letters 1914-1923.*
[89] George F. Williams to Bryan, Feb. 6, 1917, *Misc. Letters 1900-1922.*

Bryan cancelled five speaking engagements and rushed to Washington. The Zimmermann letter had just been released when he arrived at the capital, and there was little he could do save to urge his small band in Congress to cling to the war-making power with which they were vested by the Constitution.[90] He could also raise his voice in defence of the filibusterers in the Senate who were balking on the question of arming our munition-freighted ships.[91] And he could issue one final, desperate appeal to Congress. This he did on March 28,[92] mustering all his forces to make it convincing and moving. Would Congress forget that it alone could declare the war which the metropolitan press was urging on the President? Would it not remember that, cruel and unjustifiable as the wrongs inflicted on us undoubtedly were, they were not primarily directed against us? Did it make no difference that they were acts of desperation on the part of an offender who directed them against its enemies? Were we in danger of invasion? Or were we asked to send soldiers three thousand miles away to fight on others' soil? Did we not have a plan by which we had solemnly agreed to submit *all* questions to delay and inquiry? Were we to repudiate our own plan, which Germany had accepted in principle, the very first time we had an opportunity to use it? If Congress had really decided that war alone could satisfy our honor, was it too much to ask for a consultation of the wishes of the people who were to defend that honor with their lives?

Bryan had spoken, but his stock was low and his words did not alter the pattern of events. To be sure, admirers once more praised him for the boldness of his address to Congress,[93] but Congress did not listen. The Emergency Peace Federation, which had made

[90] New York *Times*, Feb. 28, Mar. 1, Mar. 2, 1917.

[91] *Ibid.*, Mar. 10, 1917.

[92] *Ibid.*, Mar. 30; *Bryan Papers*, 28.

[93] *Misc. Letters 1914-1923.* J. McK. Cattell urged Bryan to continue his vigorous appeal to the people, which alone could save them from the calamity of war; and the Socialist congressman, Meyer London, thought his services to America were comparable to those of Tolstoy to Russia. J. McK. Cattell to Bryan, Mar. 28, 1917; Louis Lochner to Bryan, Mar. 10, 1917.

his program its own,[94] was endeavoring to give his principles as wide a circulation as possible; but the cards were stacked against its efforts, which, all in all, appeared heroically pathetic.

The torrent of abuse which Bryan had experienced ever since his resignation as secretary of state had by accumulation made him feel lonely and apart. It was to be expected that the press of the great eastern cities would be as vindictive as possible; it was to be expected, too, that political foes like Roosevelt should spare no words of condemnation.[95] Nor was it a surprise when former European associates in the international movement, such as d'Estournelles de Constant, turned against him.[96] But it was a blow indeed to find his honored religious associates indicating they must disapprove of his action.[97] And it was likewise hard when old political supporters like Richard Metcalf and Senator Tillman repudiated his campaign against preparedness and openly accused him of being obsessed with the idea of "peace-at-any-price."[98] Threats to assassinate him unless he ceased talking "peace" did not of course sway him from his course, though they may well have made him uncomfortable.[99] In Baltimore an antipacifist mob yelled, "We'll hang Bill Bryan on a sour apple tree!"[100] But all this was nothing in comparison to the bitter and excessive denunciations on the floor of Congress: in February, 1917, Miller of Minnesota and Gardner of Massachusetts practically accused him of treason. He was compared to traitors and copperheads, Gardner insisting that he was tearing apart the country itself by playing politics in the midst of a national crisis.[101]   Bryan's

[94] Bryan contributed financially to the Emergency Peace Federation, but on the advice of one of its leaders did not openly affiliate with the organization lest his own effectiveness in the campaign be diminished. George W. Kirchwey to Bryan, Feb. 10, 1917, *Misc. Letters 1900-1922.*
[95] For example see New York *Times,* July 20, 1915.
[96] *Ibid.,* July 2, 1915.
[97] For example, Rev. Dr. Len G. Broughton, New York *Times,* July 19, 1915; and a letter from Bryan to Professor W. P. Trent, March 27, 1917, *Bryan Papers,* 28, *Correspondence 1915-1925.*
[98] New York *Times,* Dec. 14, 1915.
[99] Anon. to Bryan, Johnson City, Tenn., Mar. 1916, *Bryan Papers,* 28.
[100] David Starr Jordan, *The Days of a Man* (Yonkers-on-Hudson, N. Y., 1922), II, 729.
[101] *Cong. Record,* 54, Pt. 3, (64 Cong. 2 sess.) 2648, Pt. 4, 3358 (Feb. 15)

friends in the House refuted this charge by pointing out that war had not yet been declared, and that it was the right of every citizen to exercise free speech. Even a Nebraska Republican, a political enemy, rose to defend him in the interest of justice and fair play.[102]

In mid-February an effort was made to prove Bryan a violator of the Logan act, which forbids a private citizen from negotiating with a foreign Power, and to denounce him as a near-traitor. In an editorial the New York *Times* more than implied that he had inspired the dispatch of a cable, drawn up by Dr. George W. Kirchwey and Dr. George Bartholeme, to the German press, the purpose of which was to urge further concessions and explanations from Germany, and to assure its people and government that America did not want war.[103] Bryan, as a matter of fact, had no connection with this peace move other than that he had given to Dr. Kirchwey a note of introduction to a member of the cabinet, who approved the sending of the cable message. Yet Bryan was excoriated and bitterly denounced.

March came. Towards the end of the month Bryan hoped that his friends in Congress could persuade it to hear him plead against entering the war. But such consent Congress would not give. It was, as David Starr Jordan said, "pretty thoroughly hypnotized."[104] Bryan wrote to his wife from Washington:

"We are so near war that I feel that I ought to stay here—at least until tomorrow. It is distressing to see so many men afraid to act. I am needed to give them courage and help and plan."[105]

And he did urge congressmen to resign rather than to vote for war if they sincerely opposed it and yet believed it to be favored by their constituencies.[106] Beyond that he could do little save to

[102] George Huddleston to Bryan, Feb. 13, 1917, *Misc. Letters 1914-1923;* Charles A. Sloane to Bryan, Feb. 14, 1917, *Bryan Papers,* 28; New York *Times,* Feb. 14, 1917; *Cong. Record,* 54, Pt. 4, 3441, 54 Pt. 3, 2650 (Feb. 5).
[103] George W. Kirchwey to Bryan, Feb. 10, 1917. The cable is printed in the New York *Times,* Feb. 14. See also the editorial of the *Times,* "A Crime Against the Nation," Feb. 13.
[104] David Starr Jordan to Bryan, April 1, 1917, *Bryan Papers,* 34.
[105] Bryan to Mrs. Bryan (no date), *Bryan Papers,* 36.
[106] Bryan to H. C. Hilliard, Apr. 3, 1917, *Bryan Papers,* 34.

make a final appeal to the country and desperately to plan for a great, silent parade as a concrete demonstration against entering the war. The plan was for crowds to parade simultaneously in cities the length and breadth of the land. But there was no organization, either pacifist or pro-German, adequate to carry out such a project.[107] Helpless before irresistible events, he must have shared the views of his friend, Senator James Vardaman, who wrote him on March 31, 1917:

"The prospect for our country is gloomy. The advocates of preparedness have won their fight. The metropolitan newspapers have created a sentiment that seems to be sweeping the White House like a cyclone. God alone knows what will be the outcome. Your appeal is of course unanswerable and ought to have some weight—and would have great weight under different conditions. But the world has gone crazy on the subject of war and pecuniary profits." . . . (two days later) "Things look gloomy. God alone can now save this Republic, it seems to me, from the horrors of European slaughter. If the newspapers are to be believed . . . the President has made up his mind to have Congress declare war, and Congress will do his bidding."[108]

On April 5th Congress did declare war. David Starr Jordan reminded Bryan of what Norman Angell had told a group of internationalists in Europe after the cataclysm had broken out in 1914—"We were not successful, we were merely right."[109]

Right or wrong, the battle had been fought, and lost. One of his sympathetic political associates, Senator George W. Norris, has expressed the view that Bryan's opposition to the declaration of war would have been more bitter had the Republicans been in power, and that it would in that case have carried an effect impossible to understand or to measure.[110] Indeed, partisanship certainly weakened his opposition to our entry into the war: it was carried out under Democratic auspices. But it is doubtful whether the forces of opposition, which he conceivably might have

[107] George Sylvester Viereck, *Spreading Germs of Hate*, 259.
[108] James Vardaman to Bryan, March 31 and April 2, 1917, *Bryan Papers*, 34.
[109] David Starr Jordan to Bryan, April 1, 1917, *Bryan Papers*, 34.
[110] *Current History Magazine*, Sept. 1925, XXII, 865.

rallied, could have stayed the tide. In reality it was another and apparently inevitable victory of the new America over the old.

Once war was declared, Bryan's belief in the necessity of accepting the will of the majority and his patriotism made his course both clear and easy. "Please enroll me as a private whenever I am needed and assign me to any work that I can do" he wrote to President Wilson. In his editorials in *The Commoner* he favored the suspension of criticism and free speech, and he spoke out against conscientious objectors and draft resistance.[111] He contributed to the Red Cross, bought liberty bonds, and aroused patriotism among recruits at military encampments. Some of his former supporters regretted all these actions, clinging steadfastly to their convictions. Not, indeed, the American Peace Society, of which he was an officer: this organization, like Bryan, accepted the war as a holy crusade to end war.[112] But some pacifists did put personal conscience before the obligation to accept a majority decision.[113] One Unitarian minister sorrowed that Bryan could openly say that all his utterances against war, including his statement that Jesus was a pacifist, must be put on the shelf for the duration of the struggle.[114] Others, too, regretted that his peace principles seemed to apply only in time of peace, and only to foreign countries. Attorneys, editors and politicians from the West and South denounced the war in letters preserved in the Bryan papers.[115]

But Bryan's thoughts turned to peace even when he was talking war. Acting on the theory that he might be honored by an appointment to the peace commission, he spent much time in reading history, studying treaties, and otherwise preparing himself for the place he solicited of Wilson and urged senators and congress-

[111] W. G. McAdoo to Bryan, Sept. 18, 1917; Josephus Daniels to Bryan, Aug. 29, 1917, *Bryan Papers,* 34; Bryan to George Sylvester Viereck, March 15, 1921, *Bryan Papers.*
[112] Arthur Deerin Call to Bryan, June 6, 1917, *Misc. Letters 1914-1922; Advocate of Peace,* 1917-18, *passim.*
[113] George Foster Peabody to Bryan, Apr. 23, 1917, *Misc. Letters 1914-1924.*
[114] Henry W. Pinkham to Bryan, June 12, 1917, *Bryan Papers,* 34.
[115] Bryan Papers, *Misc. Letters 1914-1923,* 34.

men to help him secure.[116]   An official of the state department received his plan for handling the problem of minorities: when a territory was transferred from one Power to another, it should be so arranged that nationals might change residence without pecuniary loss.   German residents in Alsace-Lorraine, for example, who did not wish to be under French sovereignty, might sell their property to that government. While many would elect not to do so, the mere opportunity would remove much discontent and criticism.[117]   But Bryan was disappointed in his hope of being one of the peacemakers.

Bryan's position in regard to the Treaty of Versailles and the Covenant of the League of Nations was in part conditioned by his criticisms of the League to Enforce Peace.   We have seen that he denounced this organization and its principles soon after resigning as Secretary of State.[118]   The word "force," in his mind, vitiated the plan.   Peace, he had written to Bernstorff on December 15, 1916, could not be enforced: the effort to do so had been responsible for most modern wars.   It could come only as a result of the establishment of friendship and coöperation.   He could not look complacently on any plan by which America obligated herself to take part in the settlement of Europe's quarrels, even though a majority of the Council of Nations in which we were represented determined on the enforcement of its decisions in the interest of peace.[119]   He had shared Borah's idea that any participation on our part in enforcing sanctions for peace was inadvisable.[120]

When the President, in his message to Congress in January, 1917, advocated a league of nations, Bryan did not hesitate to disapprove of the implication that force was to be used to secure peace.   He told an audience in Madison, Wisconsin:[121]

[116] Bryan to Wilson, Jan. 15, 1918; J. B. Scott to Bryan, Oct. 18, 1918, *Bryan Papers*, 22.

[117] Bryan to J. B. Scott, Jan. 23, 1919, *Misc. Letters 1900-1922*.

[118] *Ante*. 224. See *World Peace*, a written debate between Wm. Howard Taft and Wm. J. Bryan. (N. Y., 1917).

[119] Bryan to Bernstorff, Dec. 15, 1916, *Bryan Papers*, 28, 1913-1925. *Memoirs of William Jennings Bryan*, 436; New York *Times*, June 20, 1915, July 3, 1915.

[120] Wm. Borah to Bryan, Dec. 29, 1916, *Bryan Papers*, 34.

[121] New York *Times*, Jan. 24, 1917.

". . . the President has sown wheat and tares together. I hope that the Senate will approve of the wheat and reject the tares."

In a newspaper article dated March 12, 1919, Bryan came out in favor of the Covenant of the League, at the same time proposing certain changes and additions. For the contemplated deliberation before war, which he identified with his own treaty plan, for the reduction of armaments, and for the abolition of secret treaties he had nothing but praise. "If the League of Nations did nothing more than provide these three things our nation would be justified in supporting it to the utmost." But he felt that the basis of representation was unfair to the United States; he favored admitting new members by a mere majority, rather than a two-thirds vote; and he advocated a clearer recognition of the Monroe Doctrine. He also desired assurance that America would not be forced to accept mandates without her consent, and that the League would not interfere in the domestic affairs of its members. Above all, each nation ought to decide for itself whether or not it would lend physical support to the undertakings and schemes of the international council. "This nation cannot afford to allow a council in which it has so small a voice to carry it into war against its will." As for the economic boycott, it was to be remembered that even such a weapon might well lead straight to war. Bryan also proposed an impractical scheme by which nations desiring "the waste places of the earth" for exploitation and expansion might acquire them peaceably through the League.[122] Yet, in spite of his objections and qualifications, he concluded that the risks we took in accepting the Covenant were less than the risk we took by rejecting it and turning back "to the old ways of blood and slaughter."

Bryan did not insist on incorporating these ideas in amendments or reservations before ratifying the Treaty and the Covenant. Indeed, he believed that it would be better to ratify first, and then to secure amendments and changes once we were a part of the League.[123] When, however, it became apparent that ratifi-

[122] David Hunter Miller, *The Drafting of the Covenant* (N. Y. and London, 1928), I, 374-7.
[123] New York *Times*, Sept. 27, 1919, Jan. 10, 1920.

cation could not be secured without reservations or amendments, then he was willing to accept many of those offered by the Republican opposition.[124]   At the Jackson Day dinner, January 9, 1920, he advocated abandoning Article X and making a compromise with the Republicans.[125]   When the President refused to listen to the idea of compromise, his representative in the Senate, Gilbert Hitchcock, asked Bryan to urge Wilson to make concessions.[126]   It was indefensible, Bryan thought, to risk the election on the question of the Covenant without reservations.[127]   Yet he did not have his way.   Administration leaders in the convention rejected the plank pledging prompt ratification with the majority reservations which he offered, and in turn Bryan withheld his support of the candidate and platform during the campaign.   Up almost to the very day of the election pleas came urging him, in the cause of international peace, to speak out for the party.[128]   He could not but think that Wilson had erred grievously and actually hindered the cause of peace.   It was his disapproval of Wilson's position on the treaty, his endorsement of universal compulsory military training and his opposition to a reduction of the army which led him later to refuse to serve on the Wilson Memorial Foundation.[129]

Disappointed in his hope that the Republicans would redeem their campaign pledge by inaugurating an "association of nations," Bryan still tried to promote machinery for peace.   He advocated our adherence to the World Court[130] and held that, since the League would probably admit us on our own terms we should not hesitate to join.[131] President Harding invited him to consult with him on our international relationships, but we do not know what

[124] Bryan to Arthur Dunn, Feb. 1, 1923, *Bryan Papers,* 28; New York *Times,* May 11, 1920.   Bryan advised Democratic senators to vote quickly for reservations, New York *Times,* Apr. 30, 1920.
[125] Dunn, *From Harrison to Harding,* II, 385; New York *Times,* Jan. 10, 1920.
[126] G. M. Hitchcock to Bryan, Nov. 30, 1919, *Bryan Papers,* 34.
[127] New York *Times,* June 27, 1920.
[128] R. W. Wooley, Sept. 24, 1920, *Bryan Papers,* 23.   Cox's "wetness" was also, of course, an important factor in Bryan's attitude.
[129] Bryan to Henry Holt, Sept. 17, 1921, *Bryan Papers,* 35.
[130] Wm. Seaver Woods to Bryan, Mar. 6, 1923, *Bryan Papers,* 19.
[131] Statement dated Apr. 24, 1923, *Bryan Papers,* 35.

took place in the interview.[132]   Efforts were later made to induce
Harding to appoint him a member of the American delegation to
the Washington Disarmament Conference,[133] but it was not to be
his fortune to contribute officially to the cause of peace. He could
only help get the churches behind the Conference, and make suggestions as to its program.   Fearing that the Four-Power treaty
might lessen our independence of action, he urged Borah, Oscar
W. Underwood and President Harding to sponsor amendments to
insure against such an eventuality.[134]   The President did not think
it necessary or wise to ask Congress to take such action.   "Of
course," wrote Harding, "you know, as I do, that there is nothing
in any of the treaties which involves us in any way, which com-
mits us to make war, which includes us in any alliance, or otherwise endangers our freedom of action."[135]

In spite of the fact that during the last years of his life his interests were chiefly in prohibition and evangelical orthodoxy,
Bryan occasionally made suggestions in the interest of world peace.
He urged on President Coolidge the cancellation of the allied
debts in the interest of better international relations, pointing out
that we might use the debts as a lever for limiting armaments.[136]
He kept up his connection with various peace and arbitration societies, contributed to a fund for the relief of the impoverished
Austrian pacifist, Alfred Fried, and supported a movement for
lessening the influence of propaganda in the press through the
establishment of an independent news bulletin.[137]   But his work
for peace was almost over.

How little his ideas on the subject of war, its causes and cure,
had been changed by the titanic struggle which he had seen, is
clearly brought out in the essay which he submitted for the Bok

[132] Harding to Bryan, Nov. 13, 1920, *Bryan Papers*, 35.

[133] Mrs. Harding to Mrs. Bryan, July 28, 1921, *Bryan Papers*, 19.

[134] Borah to Bryan, Dec. 13, 1921, *Bryan Papers*, 23; Oscar W. Underwood to Bryan, Mar. 14, 1922, *Misc. Papers 1914-1923;* Bryan to Harding,
Jan. 26, 1922, *Bryan Papers*, 35.

[135] Harding to Bryan, Jan. 31, 1922, *Bryan Papers*, 35.

[136] Bryan to Coolidge, Jan. 1, 1925, Coolidge to Bryan, Jan. 5, 1925, *Misc.
Papers 1923-6.*

[137] *Bryan Papers*, 24.

prize. His draft distinguished between justiciable and non-justiciable disputes. The former were to be submitted to the existing international court; the latter, without exception, were to be referred to commissions of inquiry. All legal and moral obligation to use force in carrying out the decisions was repudiated, although nations might, by international agreement, refuse loans and commercial intercourse to governments that began war without first submitting the dispute to the court or commissions of inquiry. And in no instance, save actual invasion, was war to be declared save by popular referendum. In addition to these familiar ideas, the plan emphasized the necessity of developing peace sentiment through meetings, discussion of the causes and cure of war, extension of woman suffrage throughout the world, and the naming of highways in such a manner as to suggest peace. This plan, which was submitted under a pseudonym, failed to win the prize. Deprived of that consolation Bryan sent the paper to President Coolidge and to Secretary of State Kellogg to whom he wrote, by way of an explanation for sending his essay, "As you know, my heart has been in the peace movement for nearly a quarter of a century."[138] This is the last statement of Bryan's interest in peace to be found in his papers. Three months later he was dead.

[138] Bryan to Kellogg, May 1, 1925, *Bryan Papers,* 35.

CONCLUSION

Long after Bryan's death, and probably long after the passing of all his contemporaries, others will fight his battle for peace. Hard as that fight will be, it cannot but be somewhat easier because of this conscientious and intelligent critic of the war system who was, after all, a pioneer among political authorities in experimenting with concrete machinery for preventing war.

Some will continue to fight for peace in his way; others will find different, and perhaps better, ways. From his mistakes all warriors against war can learn lessons of value. For those who, like him, will continue to emphasize the Christian and individualistic approach, the best lesson he can teach is the weakness of inconsistency. Pacifists who approach the problem from the point of view of doctrinaire opposition to war under *all* possible circumstances, will attribute Bryan's failure to his willingness to regard war as the last desperate, inevitable means to an end. They will tell us that the fatal weakness in his tactics was his acceptance of war as an exceptional and "holy crusade" once his country opened the gates of Janus. Bryan's tragedy was, in their estimation, due to the fact that he went so far towards the position of consistently refusing to sanction war, and yet, when the time of testing came, attached a higher value to nationalism than to peace. Their warning will be for friends of peace to steel themselves against the kind of rationalizations by which Bryan was able to talk peace in time of peace, and make war in time of war.

Others who would have us learn a lesson from Bryan's failure will insist that those who really want peace must recognize the futility of an individualistic morality in a society so complex and so ordered, economically, as to be blind to the sort of appeal that may still be effective when made to individuals. Those who approach the problem from the socialist point of view will insist that if Bryan's mistakes are not to be repeated, friends of peace must do even more than see some of the connections between capitalism and war; they will do more than denounce the war propaganda of a profit-minded press; they will not stop with criticism of munition-makers and bankers profiting from lending neutral resources to belligerents; they will not even pin their faith to a popular referendum on the question of war or peace. They will realize that the people, influenced by propaganda, are not always right; that they are, in short, the victim of agencies and forces over which they have, at present, no effective control. They will take a more realistic view of human nature. Bryan, these critics will tell us, wanted peace, but at the same time wanted other things which were incompatible with peace, and, in the last analysis, wanted them more than he wanted peace. If enemies of war would learn from Bryan's failures, they must take the profits out of the whole system which has bred so many wars; they must so order society that one class, and one nation, cannot exploit another class, and another nation. For so long as that can be done, may it not be said that the instruments for exploitation will be found? Bryan's tragedy, these critics would say, was that he came so near to seeing these relationships, and was yet blinded, in the time of testing, by a more fundamental loyalty to private property and its legal rights.

Bryan was, in a tragic sense, the champion of lost causes, or, at least, of causes that appear half-lost: free silver, anti-imperialism, effective prohibition, and anti-evolution. But, more than any person in his day, he put these causes, together with that of world peace, before the people. It is yet to be decided whether world peace shall be added to the list of causes for which he fought—and which were lost.

BIBLIOGRAPHY

I

Manuscripts

In the summer of 1929 the *Bryan Papers* in the Library of Congress were still largely in the original cartons in which they were received. Citations to the papers follow the titles which the cartons then carried. Often, however, papers were found in cartons which were not relevant to their titles. The papers were not well classified. The *Woodrow Wilson Letterbook* contained carbon copies of a large number of the letters Bryan wrote to Wilson while secretary of state. In general, however, the papers contain disappointingly few carbons or first drafts of Bryan's letters. Mrs. W. W. Bailey and Dr. Charles Macfarland kindly sent me originals or copies of Bryan letters in their possession.

II

Autobiographies, Correspondence and Writings

Baker, Ray Stannard, and Dodd, William E., *The Public Papers of Woodrow Wilson*, (N. Y., 1926) I-IV.

Bartholdt, Richard, *From Steerage to Congress*, (Phil., 1930).

Bernstorff, Count Johann von, *My Three Years in America*, (N. Y., 1920).

Bryan, Mary Baird, *The Memoirs of William Jennings Bryan*, (Phil., 1925).

Bryan, William Jennings, *British Rule in India*, (London, 1906).

Bryan, William Jennings, *In His Image*, (N. Y., 1922).

Bryan, William Jennings, *Speeches*, (N. Y. and London, 1913) II.

Bryan, William Jennings, *The Old World and Its Ways*, (St. Louis, 1907).

Bryan, William Jennings, *The Second Battle*, (Chicago, 1900).

Bryan, William Jennings, *Under Other Flags*, (Lincoln, 1905).

Butt, Archibald Wellington, *Taft and Roosevelt. The Intimate Letters of Archie Butt*, (N. Y., 1930) I-II.

Carnegie, Andrew, *Autobiography*, (Boston and N. Y., 1920).

Daniels, Josephus, "Wilson and Bryan," *Saturday Evening Post*, Sept. 5, 1925, 54 ff.

Dumba, Constantin, *Memoirs of a Diplomat*, (Boston, 1932).

Gwynn, Stephen, *The Letters and Friendships of Sir Cecil Spring-Rice*, (London, 1929) I-II.

Harrison, Frederick, *Autobiographic Memories*, (London, 1911) I-II.

256   Smith College Studies in History

Hendrick, Burton J., *Life and Letters of Walter Hines Page,* (Garden City, 1922-1925) I-III.
Hoar, George F., *Autobiography of Seventy Years,* (N. Y., 1903) I-II.
Houston, David F., *Eight Years in Wilson's Cabinet,* (N. Y., 1926) I-II.
Jordan, David Starr, *The Days of a Man,* (Yonkers-on-Hudson, 1922) I-II.
Lansing, Robert, "The Difficulties of Neutrality," *Saturday Evening Post,* April 18, 1931.
Lochner, Louis P., *America's Don Quixote,* (London, 1924).
McAdoo, William G., *Crowded Years,* (Boston and N. Y., 1931).
Pettigrew, R. F., *Imperial Washington,* (Chicago, 1922).
Redfield, William C., *With Congress and Cabinet,* (N. Y., 1924).
Selections from the Correspondence of Theodore Roosevelt and Henry Cabot Lodge, (N. Y., 1925) I-II.
Seymour, Charles, *The Intimate Papers of Colonel House,* (Boston, 1926) I-II.
Straus, Oscar S., *Under Four Administrations,* (Boston, 1922).
Taft, William Howard, *The United States and World Peace,* (N. Y., 1914).
Tolstoy, Count Leo, "Bethink Yourselves," *The Living Age,* 242 (1904).
Tumulty, Joseph P., *Woodrow Wilson as I Know Him,* (N. Y., 1921).
Viereck, George Sylvester, *Spreading Germs of Hate,* (N. Y., 1930).

III

United States Government Documents

Congressional Record.
Foreign Relations of the United States, 1913, 1914, 1914 Supplement, 1915, 1915 Supplement.

IV

Unofficial Documents

Democratic Campaign Book, Presidential Election, 1900, (Washington, 1900).
Official Report of the XIV Universal Peace Conference, (London, 1907).
Proceedings of the National Arbitration and Peace Congress in New York, (N. Y., 1907).
Report of the Sixteenth Annual Meeting of the Lake Mohonk Conference, "The Forces that Make for Peace," (1910).

*Résolutions Textuelles des Congres Universels de la Paix tenus
de 1843 à 1910,* (Berne, 1912).
*Sessional Proceedings of National Association for the Promotion
of Social Science for the year 1870-1871,* (London, 1871).
Union Interparlementaire XIII e conference, (Bruxelles, 1905).

V

NEWSPAPERS

Boston *Globe,* 1898.
London *Times,* 1914.
New York *American,* 1915.
New York *Evening Post,* 1915.
New York *Herald,* 1915.
New York *Sun,* 1915.
New York *Times,* 1898, 1913-1920, 1928.
New York *Tribune,* 1898.
New York *World,* 1915-1916.
Philadelphia *Record,* 1915.
Springfield *Republican,* 1898, 1913.
Washington *Herald,* 1915.

VI

PERIODICALS

Advocate of Peace, The, 1874, 1900, 1913-1915, 1917-1918.
Arbitrator, The, 1914, (London).
Christian Herald, The, 1915.
Commoner, The, 1905, 1906, 1914.
Concord, 1914-1915.
Herald of Peace, The, 1914, (London).
Independent, The, 1904, 1906.
La Paix par le Droit, 1913-1914.
Literary Digest, "The Allies' New Bond", 49, Sept. 19, 1914.
Peacemaker, The, 1893, 1900.
Völker-Friede, 1913.
War and Peace, (The International Review), 1914, (London).

SECONDARY MATERIALS

American Secretaries of State and Their Diplomacy, "William
Jennings Bryan," Anon., Vol. X, (N. Y., 1929).
Baker, Ray Stannard, *Woodrow Wilson, Life and Letters,* (N. Y.,
1931) III-IV.
Beard, Charles and Mary, *The Rise of American Civilization,* (N.
Y., 1927) II.
Croly, Herbert, *Willard Straight,* (N. Y., 1925).

Curti, M. E., *The American Peace Crusade 1815-1860,* (Durham 1929).

Daniels, Joseph, *The Life of Woodrow Wilson,* (Chicago and Philadelphia, 1924).

Davis, Jerome, *Contemporary Social Movements,* (N. Y., 1930).

Dunn, Arthur Wallace, *From Harrison to Harding,* (N. Y. and London, 1922) I-II.

Field, Henry M., *The Life of David Dudley Field,* (N. Y., 1898).

Foreign Policy Association, "The Seizure of Haiti by the United States", (N. Y., 1922).

Hibben, Paxton, *The Peerless Leader,* (N. Y., 1929).

Howe, M. A. DeWolf, *James Ford Rhodes,* (N. Y., 1929).

Knight, Melvin M., *The Americans in Santo Domingo,* (N. Y., 1928).

Lange, Christian L., *The American Peace Treaties,* (Kristiania, 1915).

Lawrence, David, *The True Story of Woodrow Wilson,* N. Y., 1924).

Marshall, Helen Edith, *The Social Philosophy of William Jennings Bryan,* (Master's Thesis, University of Chicago, 1929).

Miller, David Hunter, *The Drafting of the Covenant,* (N. Y. and London, 1928) I-II.

Norris, George K., "Bryan as a Political Leader," *Current History Magazine,* XXII, Sept., 1925.

Putnam, George Haven, "Theodore Roosevelt, Boy and Man," *Review of Reviews,* LIX, Jan., 1919, 153-155.

Shaw, Albert, "William Jennings Bryan," *Review of Reviews,* LXXII, Aug., 1925, 259-263.

Shotwell, James T., *War as an Instrument of National Policy,* (N. Y., 1929).

The Inter-Parliamentary Union, Its Work and Organization, 3 ed., (Geneva, 1930).

Villard, Fanny Garrison, *William Lloyd Garrison on Non-Resistance,* (N. Y., 1924).

Welles, Sumner, *Naboth's Vineyard,* (N. Y., 1928) I-II.

Werner, M. R., *Bryan,* (N. Y., 1929).

Woolsey, Theodore D., *Communism and Socialism in their History and Theory,* (London, 1879).

World Peace Foundation Pamphlets, 1912, 1916, (Boston).

INDEX

Addams, Jane, 190
Advocate of Peace, on Bryan, quoted, 171; on Wilson, quoted, 179
Aguinaldo, on Bryan, quoted, 134
American Neutral Conference Committee, 241
American Peace Society, 115, 247
Americans on British Ships, 198 ff
Anglo-American Peace Centenary, 170
Angell, Norman, 153, 246
Anti-Imperialist League, 133

Ballou, Adin, 136
Barrett, John, 240
Bartholdt, Richard, 145, 221
Bartholeme, Dr. George, 245
Bernstorff, Count Johann von, and Bryan's Treaties, 156
Blymyer, William, 144
Bok Prize, 251
Borah, William, 248, 251
Brisbane, Arthur, 128-129
Bryan Treaties, Netherlands, 151; Salvador, 151; New York *Times,* quoted on, 153; London *Evening Standard,* quoted on, 154; London *Review,* quoted on, 154; London *Times,* quoted on, 154; influence of, 161 ff
Bryan, William Jennings, devotion to party, 114, 183; influence of Christianity on, 114, 130; influence of American individualism on, 115; faith in democracy, 116; philosophy of peace, not original, 116; as a military officer, 118; as Secretary of State, 150 ff; inconsistency in attitude towards dollar diplomacy and economic imperialism, 177; loyalty to Democratic Party, 183, 246; attitude towards belligerents, 193; resignation from Cabinet, 217 ff; work in chautauqua, 228 ff; plans for going to Europe to end the war, 230-233; attacks on, 244 ff; supports World War after America enters, 247; World Court, 250
Bryce, Lord, 147
Burton, Senator Theodore, 155

Campbell-Bannerman, Sir Henry, 145, 148
Canal Tolls Exemption Act, 157
Carnegie, Andrew, 122, 124, 127 ff; quoted, 152 f; 182
Carranza, 181
Central American Conference, 163
Chautauqua, Bryan's part in, 134, 141-142, 167 and f
China, Bryan's policy towards, 184 ff; Six-Power loan to, 184
Chinda, Ambassador, 186, 221 f
Christianity, Bryan on, 119, 139
Colombia, 176
Commission of Inquiry, 145 ff
Commoner, The, 134, 141
Contraband, United States and, 198 and f
Coolidge, Calvin, 251
Cremer, Sir Randal, 147
Cushing, The, 210, 213

Daniels, Josephus, 156
Declaration of London, 194
Democracy, Bryan and, 130
Democratic Party and Imperialism, 125 ff
Democratic Platform of 1900, Bryan and, 132
Democrats, on Expansion, 121
Disarmament, Bryan on, 168
Dollar Diplomacy, Bryan's relation to, 176-177
Dumas, Jacques, 153
Dumba, Dr. Constantin, 156
"Dumba Incident", 204 ff

Edward, King, 148
Embargo on Munitions, 180-181, 194 ff, 197-198, 227-228
Emergency Peace Federation, 243 ff